RATIONAL ECONOMICS

RATIONAL ECONOMICS

by
Robin Jackson

Philosophical Library
New York

Library of Congress Cataloging-in-Publication Data

Jackson, Robin.
  Rational economics.

  1. Capitalism.   2. Economics.   3. Rand, Ayn.
I. Title.
HB501.J27   1987   330.1   86-30260
ISBN 0-8022-2529-2

Copyright 1987 by Philosophical Library, Inc.
200 West 57th Street, New York, N.Y. 10019

Manufactured in the United States of America

Contents

Part I
Rational Economics

Chapter I

Who Decides?

Economics, the study of the production and distribution by man of goods and services, differs from the natural sciences in an important way. All sciences including economics deal with man's external world; economics must also contend with certain aspects of man's behavior. Man's thoughts and actions are irrelevant to the chemist, but critical to the economist. Therefore the development of rational economics presupposes an understanding of man's nature and behavior.

This understanding depends on the resolution of

3

three issues. One must understand the nature of man himself. One must understand man's relationship with the external world. One must understand man's relationship with his fellow man. Only after these questions are answered can economic science define concepts and discover general truths.

The concerns raised above arise in many other contexts. They are important, wide-ranging issues which affect large areas of human thought. For this reason they are the subject of a specialized field of study: philosophy. Philosophy is the generalized study of being, knowledge, and conduct. It provides the conceptual framework necessary to understand man's behavior; hence, the study of economics presumes a previous study of philosophy.

Three areas of philosophy relate directly to economics. First, what is man's nature? What makes him different from other living beings in particular and other existents in general? What essential defining characteristics do all men share? Second, what is man's relationship to the external world? How does he perceive it, understand it, and survive in it? Third, what is the nature of the relationship among men? Does the difference between a man and, say, a rock require that one differentiate the two as objects of one's actions? If so, how? What is the essential difference? Which actions among men are proper and which are immoral?

Before one attempts any economics, these questions must be answered. The validity of the answers determines the validity of the resultant economics. Perhaps these questions appear irrelevant to economics. However, it has been precisely the lack of correct answers that has invalidated most economics.

Aristotle stated that man is a rational animal. Two

thousand years have not improved this definition. Man is the only known living being that must exercise reason to survive. Decisions must be made, for man has no inherent patterns of behavior and no instincts to guide him. He must develop an understanding of his environment before he can live successfully in it. The essential characteristic that makes an animal a man is rationality—that is, possessing the faculty of reason.

The mechanism which exercises rationality, the human mind, has one outstanding characteristic: it is a primary, indivisible unit. The quantum of human intelligence is the individual; the word "ego" exists in recognition of this fact. Two men cannot share one mind any more than they can share one body.

Modern physics provides a useful analogy. This science would now be defunct if it did not recognize the existence of a primary, indivisible unit of energy: the quantum. The realization and acceptance of this truth led to the development of lasers and computers. Physics remains a growing, vital science because it attempts to discover, not dispute, the truth.

Similarly, philosophy must recognize that human beings are and act as individuals. The abilities to decide and to reason are attributes of the human mind, and of no other known entity. The collective will and the collective decision-making process do not exist; they are non-concepts. A group of individuals may reach a partial or complete consensus regarding some issue; that is a statement about the action of individual men, not a demonstration of a holistic group will. The claim that membership in some group, however defined, allows or requires the group to expropriate its members' decision-making ability is nonsense. Any man can always decide to act differently from his peers. This action may exact a cost as great as his life, but the alternative always exists. Men function and make decisions as individuals, and only individuals can make decisions. For philosophy to remain a science, philosophers must appreciate and accept these truths.

Man is a rational animal. This statement defines man, for no other known entity possesses these characteristics.

Man's relationship with his external world[1] is one of existence; he either exists in it or he does not. To survive in this world man must perceive it, understand it, and act upon it. Within the context of man the decision-maker, the issue breaks into two parts: how does man make decisions? How does man use decisions to enhance his survival?

The human mind, in common with the minds of other animals, receives information about the world via the senses. These sensory data cause a perception in the mind, a perception that always corresponds to a tangible existent. A perception is the integration of diverse sensory data into a mental unit corresponding to a unit in reality. Man goes beyond the animals in that he mentally organizes his perceptions in an efficient, logical manner by integrating them into categories through the use of concepts.

"A concept is an abstract mental integration of two or more units which are isolated according to a specific characteristic and united by a specific definition. The

---

[1] For lack of a better term, we define "nature" to be the entire physical universe with the exception of man. Hence, the universe consists of the two mutually exclusive and mutually exhaustive categories: man and nature. This terminology is somewhat unfortunate, because "nature" is an overworked term. Specifically, this book will have "nature" doing double duty, meaning also the essential character of an entity, as in "the nature of man" (sic). The appropriate meaning will be clear from the context.

units involved may be any aspect of reality: entities, attributes, actions, qualities, relationships, etc.; they may be perceptual concretes or other earlier-formed concepts."[2]

Concepts are the assemblies and sub-assemblies with which the mind engineers the mental organization of its perception of reality. Concepts are created through man's ability to reason. As an intellectual tool, concepts enable man both to know more about his environment and to increase that knowledge more easily. An individual is the only known entity that can conceptualize.

The simplest examples of concepts are those that integrate tangible existents. If primitive man had to assign a separate name to every particular animal he hunted and to every particular plant he harvested (as we now give a specific name, the proper name, to every human individual), his mental processes would succumb to a sea of irrelevant detail, and hence his food-producing activities would grind to a halt. His survival would suffer and possibly cease. It is not important, for the purpose of survival, which particular stalk of wheat he harvest, only that he harvest wheat. Wheat is the name he gives to the concept which abstracts the important features of all existing individual wheat plants—i.e., that they are edible plants that will sustain his existence if used in a certain manner. The use of the concept wheat enables him to store efficiently the important facts concerning many individual wheat plants, and hence enhance his knowledge of nature.

One uses concepts to understand the nature of the real world. Through their use, a man can know more

---

[2] A. Rand, *Introduction to Objectivist Epistemology* (Mentor, 1979), p. 11.

than he has individually perceived. The knowledge concepts encompass is the first component necessary in making decisions.

A decision is not required until a goal has been undertaken. Goals originate from fundamental requirements of survival: food, clothing, and shelter. In more advanced societies, goals are less directly connected to these basic requirements, but connected nonetheless. An identified goal is the second component necessary in making decisions.

Once understanding is achieved and goals identified, man uses his conceptual knowledge of reality to create potential strategies (courses of action) which might be used to reach his goal. His reason deduces the consequences and outcomes of each strategy. He then evaluates outcomes within the context of enhancement of his survival and makes his decision. There is no guarantee that the decision taken will be, in some objective sense, the right or best one. The decision's value will depend on the individual's knowledge, intelligence, values, and effort.

A prosaic example demonstrating this process is the dilemma of a high school graduate: should he commence work immediately or invest in four years of college? Suppose his goal is the achievement of a satisfactory income via meaningful employment. To make a rational decision he must first develop a conceptual understanding of each alternative. He can obtain this through direct observation (attending sample college classes, talking to individuals who chose work after high school) or indirect observation (reading books on the subject). This understanding may lead to further possible alternatives—i.e., work for two years and then attend college. After understanding the alternatives and their consequences, he would weigh each according to his personal estimate of its value to him. Comparing these values he may decide to attend college immediately.

Note that at this point, no action has been taken: the decision is strictly a mental activity.

Hence the ability to make decisions has four prerequisites. An individual must perceive and understand his environment through the use of his senses and the mental device of concepts. He must formulate and identify goals that, if achieved, enhance his survival. He must create and evaluate alternative courses of action. He must choose that alternative which best realizes his goal. Only then is a decision made.

This process of decision-making can be conceptually integrated into a mental process called reason. It is the first half of man's means of survival.

A decision, being abstract and intangible, is of no use to further one's survival unless it results in action. If not translated to action, decisions fall into the realm of daydreams. Only because man's mind controls the actions of his body can he implement decisions. The body translates the mind's decisions into action and physical reality.

As an integrated being of mind and body, man survives by concretizing abstract decisions. Such is his only means of affecting nature.

In the example of the high school student, this action takes the form of sending letters to several colleges requesting curriculum information.

Man's relationship with nature has two components. Man combines his understanding, achieved by organizing his perceptions into concepts, with the goals he sets, resulting in mental decisions. Man concretizes these abstract decisions, acting on nature with his body, which his mind controls. Man invents the lever by observing its principle in nature, then uses it to move the mountain of his choice.

Men differ from all elements of nature in so profound a manner that the relationship between men does not resemble the relationship discussed above between man and nature. This difference stems from man's ability and need to make decisions. A man who sets fire to a pile of logs evokes a different reaction than one who sets fire to another man. The relationship between two men is a relationship between two identically defined entities (not identified entities—this difference distinguishes equality and egalitarianism); the relationship between a man and nature is not. Nature does not concretize abstract decisions for the simple reason it does not make decisions. Earthquakes do not choose their victims. Men do.

A man in isolation is free to do, say, and think as he pleases. The only standard by which his actions can be judged is their effectiveness in enhancing his survival as a living, reasoning being: how well do they aid his purpose of living here on earth?

The situation of two men isolated together imposes a constraint on the actions of each. Ideally, both men should be free to do, say, and think as they please, because this freedom is the metaphysical means on which their survival depends. Here, means refer to the general, abstract principle involved, not the day-to-day, concrete minutiae. This freedom is the moral prerequisite for men to possess the possibility of survival (it does not guarantee survival, for we shall see there is no automatic way to do so). However, both men cannot be completely free in action, for there exists the case in which one man is the object of the second man's action. In such a case, actions that impair the ability of the first man to make or concretize decisions cannot be permitted. No other actions can be forbidden because that would impair the second's ability to act beyond what is metaphysically necessary.

This situation generalizes readily to society. A man in society must be free[3] to decide and do as he wishes provided his actions do not physically impair the abilities of others to do the same. In practical terms, this means men should not initiate violence (actual or threatened) on each other's persons. The unilateral use of force is wrong.[4]

A man can do what he wishes to a rock. The rock does not and cannot care. To care implies a decision between good and bad; ultimately the alternatives of life or death. The rock is not capable of decision, nor of experiencing life or death. In contrast, a man cannot morally do as he wishes to another man. The second man does care about the nature of that action because he is a decision-making entity and because his survival as such may depend on that action.

The essential difference between men and other existents is man's rational consciousness. If the object of one's action is a man, then it is wrong to initiate the use of force or violence. If the object of one's action is other than a man, then no such restriction applies.

Our exploration of the relevant philosophical issues has answered the questions posed at the beginning of this section. To apply these ideas to economics, we must condense them to a small number of principles which summarize all necessary information. They must be further conceptualized so that one can use them efficiently.

The absolute necessity for consistency and the sym-

---

[3] The guarantor of freedom is the government.

[4] The retaliatory use of force is another matter and is not relevant here.

metry of the relationship between any two men lead to the following.

A man should be (it is moral that a man is) free to decide (think) and to concretize decisions (do, move, speak) subject only to the limitation that he not initiate the use of actual or threatened violence or force on another man. This limitation objectively prevents men from interfering with each other's survival mechanisms and is the only moral means for doing so. This is man's inalienable right to his own life, a right that inheres in his very nature.

The unit standard of value of this ethics is man (as opposed to society or a god or the state).

That human right encompasses a great deal of the preceding philosophy. However, it does not state, but merely implies, a result of extreme importance to economics: the method whereby the simultaneous relationships of several men with nature are managed.

Men survive by concretizing decisions, that is, by willfully acting upon real objects. What if two men independently decide to act simultaneously on the same object? The only available physical solution is the use of force; however, the result we have just referred to precludes a violent resolution. Merely banning the use of force is not a solution. In addition to specifying what cannot be done, one must also say what is to be done. A resolution is necessary for two reasons. One, the situation will occur with certainty in a finite world. Two, survival requires that decisions be translated into action.

Because a physical solution is not moral, men must devise an abstract one. Because all men are equally valid referents of the concept man, there is no a priori reason to favor one man's decision over another in a given situation. Hence the situation must be prevented from occurring. The only way to achieve that is the assignment (one-to-one correspondence) of real existents to men. The problem of simultaneous acts on the same object is resolved by preventing its existence. For a given existent at a given time, there must exist one and only one man with the privilege of acting on it. This assignment of men to existents is, among other things, a function of time. At a given juncture, the assignment is fixed.

Any other method of assignment, or lack of any assignment, will lead to either violence or inaction, and hence death.

Property is any existent in nature that has been assigned to some individual. That individual is the only person who can morally act upon that existent. No other individual can morally concretize a decision on that object. The assigned individual is said to be the owner of the property. The relationship between the man and the property is one of ownership. From the previous discussion of human rights, it is evident that no man can be considered another man's property.

These ideas can be summarized in the following concept: the right of property ownership.

It is right that for every known tangible existent, there exist a corresponding individual, the owner, with the exclusive right to have, use and dispose of that existent as he sees fit. This correspondence consists of a recognition that only one man may have the right to act (to concretize decisions) on a given existent. This right stems from the following truths: men must concretize decisions to survive; the initiation of violence toward men is immoral; and decisions are an attribute of individuals and no other known entity.

The right to property is a statement explaining the simultaneous relationships of man with nature. It does not state that any given individual must own a certain amount of property (or indeed any). It is a moral statement, not an economic one. Its raison d'etre is the prevention of violence, while allowing the concretization of decisions. Without the right to property a man cannot be free, for he must then depend on some other agent (dictator, government agency, aristocrat) to act on his immediate environment in such a way as to continue his survival, and he cannot be guaranteed that that agent will act in his interest. The right to property stems from the decision-making ability of humans. The existence of the property concept is solely dependent on the existence of decisions. In isolation a rock is a rock and nothing more. It becomes property only when a man decides to smelt it, mine it, build with it, or crush it.

If one ignores the truth that the definition of man imposes a symmetry on all men (all men are equally valid referents of the concept man), then one is forced into somehow defining a group of elitist decision-makers. All racism originates in this way. Racism is irrational and immoral, and can be sustained only through the illegitimate use of force as a proxy for the decisions expropriated from the oppressed individuals. Racism artificially segments men into at least two classes: those who have property rights and those who do not. No moral justification for this action exists. The right of property ownership by the individual is a prerequisite for avoiding racism and for establishing morality.

Men own what they buy, trade for, or produce. All stem from man's right to decide his property's fate, including the possibility of assigning its ownership to another willing individual. Men can create complex joint forms of ownership and associations such as corporations and partnerships, consisting of the mutual agreement to joint ownership of property through the device of abstract legal entities. Two requirements exist. One, there must be willful agreement by all involved parties. Two, a procedure must be specified in advance to make and concretize decisions involving the jointly owned property. Similarly, one man can temporarily assign ownership to another willing man through trusteeship. The legal forms of property are limited only by the imagination and the two requirements above. This distinguishes property from the expropriation of decision-making by force as practiced by states and some elitist individuals.

The moral source of property is the decision-making ability of the individual. Because this source is inherent in the nature of man, it is an inalienable right; government does not grant him this right, it secures it for him. All property is private property. Public property is a contradiction in terms; the public is not a decision-making entity. The public's so-called right to property is not inalienable, but merely a granted privilege.

The philosophic background required to study economics can be summarized by the two existing human rights. In actuality, the second is a corollary of the first.

It is right that a man is free to decide and concretize decisions subject only to the limitation that he not initiate actual or threatened violence on another man's body. It is right that there exist a one-to-one correspondence between all individuals and all tangible existents except man. This correspondence consists of the exclusive right to act on a given existent.

There are no other human rights.[5] All other supposed human rights stem from one or more of the following

---

[5] Note that the first right specifies what man cannot do. By implication, there are innumerable things he can do: freely speak, freely trade, pursue happiness, etc.

defects in logic. They ignore the nature of man. They ignore that all men are equally valid referents of the concept man. They ignore man's relationship with nature.

The right to property is so fundamental to the study of economics that it is important to understand how previous economists have come to err concerning the nature of property.

Political philosophers ascribe the faculty of ownership to an entity other than an individual; for example, to a group of individuals or society in general, as in public property. Modern society abounds with arbitrarily defined groups of individuals that enjoy certain legally enforced rights to property not available to individuals. Examples include: unions which have the legal right to restrain trade; ethnic groups with legal claims to education or employment; legislative groups with the right to practice legal extortion (the forcible expropriation of an individual's property); and legal monopolies such as utilities with the legal right to prevent individuals from entering their businesses as a competitor. These examples, while not exhaustive, illustrate the pervasiveness of invalid economic thought.

The supposition of group rights leads directly to two non-resolvable problems. One, what constitutes a group? What individual defines the extent of a group and on what basis is this individual chosen? How can one prevent the inconsistencies and conflicts arising from the competing "rights" of different groups? Two, how can one morally justify the idea that the rights an individual possesses depend on what particular group(s) he is allied with? What moral or practical reason exists for granting a right to one individual and denying it to another?

Only force can answer these questions, not logic. The reason rights exist (individual man's decision-making nature) simply does not apply to any group of individuals, however chosen. Hence, no group, as a group, has the right to property.

The contradictions inherent in group property rights become obvious if one considers the most limiting case: socialism or communism (which are one and the same). Under either, one supergroup, society, owns everything. The State makes all decisions concerning property. In practice, the State consists of a group of elite individuals who have expropriated all property (a direct admission that no such thing as a decision-making group exists—individuals must make the decisions). Socialism does not evade the need for property or property rights—decisions must be made and concretized in order that man can survive. Socialism merely distills this decision-making into an elite class of individuals.

That this elite may have been selected democratically is irrelevant. The power of a State and the selection of its leaders are two distinct issues. It is certainly possible and moral for an individual to assign his ownership of certain property to a willing trustee of his choice. To be forced to do so by threatened violence is not moral. Democracy is merely one of several possible methods of choosing the leaders of a State. A State's democratic-ness is independent of its powers, moral premises, or treatment of property rights.

The usual justification for socialism, or for public property, is based on so-called human needs of individuals or groups. One uses the automatic assumption that all needs must be satisfied to justify the extortion of private property. One ignores the questions: what is a human need, why must they be automatically satisfied, what guarantee exists that the means of satisfaction can be found, who judges the extent of needs, who has the authority to impose his will on others, and what is the responsibility of individuals to satisfy their own needs, however defined? Naturally, life's necessities expand to use up the available production and then some. However, the act of defining some product as necessary does not guarantee its existence. Transfer does not equal production.

Economically, socialism does not work because it ignores reality, specifically production. Morally, socialism divides humanity into two classes: those with property rights and those without, and hence is racist. Metaphysically, socialism is a futile attempt to find some automatic, effortless method of survival without the responsibility of decision-making. The result: either a cold-blooded dictatorship (the Soviet Union) or economic paralysis (Great Britain).

It is right that all men be free to decide and to concretize decisions, subject only to the limitation that they do not initiate the use of actual or threatened violence on another man.

This implies the right to property ownership. It is right that there exists a one-to-one correspondence between individuals and all known tangible existents excluding man. This correspondence consists of limiting the right to act on a given existent to one and only one man. This right is the only possible moral mechanism that reconciles the need of all men to survive by concretizing decisions with the need to avoid the initiation of violence on men.

A claim to any other rights is logically inconsistent. This means that if any of these "rights" is applied, one can always create a situation in which contradictions of unanswerable questions exist. Usually these so-called rights either divide men into arbitrary classes (for irrelevant reasons) or assume that production is automatic.

Capitalism is the political system premised on inalienable individual rights: the right to life and the right to property. The function of government in a capitalist society is to secure these rights for all individuals. The mechanism used is a government monopoly on the use of physical coercion directed at individuals who abuse others' rights. The safeguard which regulates the actions of government is an objective judicial system, a system based on principles and laws, not on opinions and the wills of individuals.

The smallness of current intellectual thought is indicated by its consideration of capitalism as merely an (outmoded) economic system. This characterization logically implies the non-primacy of individual rights, although its proponents usually do not explicitly state this implication. Modern intellectuals set up and attack a straw man they pass off as capitalism. America's future depends on its intellectuals rediscovering the true nature of capitalism.

Capitalism, thus defined, has never been practiced anywhere, at any time in history. Nineteenth-century America was as close as man has come. Capitalism has been condemned without a trial. The worldwide trend to statism has continued throughout the entire twentieth century and, if unchecked, will destroy civilization and plunge mankind into another Dark Ages.

Chapter Two

Wealth and Trade

Man's ability to make decisions derives from his understanding of his world; his ability to act on those decisions depends on his immediate physical environment. For an individual in isolation, therefore, his ability to survive depends on two factors: the extent of his knowledge (and mental ability to use that knowledge) and the nature, extent, and value of his property. The latter is often called natural resources—a poor name, for resources are resources only if one knows what to do with them. The oil, coal, and uranium the American

20

Indian lived over for thousands of years were valueless to him.

We call the extent of one's ability to survive one's wealth. Wealth is the wherewithal to command nature. For an isolated individual, one's wealth is a function of one's knowledge and one's property.

Wealth must be distinguished from power. In the context of economics, power is the ability to forcibly dominate other individuals. One possesses power in great measure if one is able to forcibly dominate (whether through legal means such as government or other means) many individuals. The wealthy command nature, the powerful command men.

Power without wealth is of little value to enhance survival. All the laws and orders one can issue will not produce a single product nor explain a single cause. A society consisting of politicians and bureaucrats would starve immediately. People who exercise power need producers as the object of that power. Unfortunately for the powerful, producers tend to exist in inverse proportion to the number of powerful. A great many civilizations learned this fact the hard way.

In the real world, men do not live in isolation; hence we must learn how membership in society affects one's wealth. It is an obvious empirical fact that a particular man's ability to survive depends largely on which particular society he belongs to. The life expectancy and quality of life in modern America are far greater than, for example, in most African countries or in societies prior to this century. By today's standards, the vast majority of all people that ever existed lived short, cruel lives.

The lack of a historical perspective causes misconceptions about wealth. People tend to measure their wealth against those around them, rather than against their forefathers. This relative measure, in place of the objective standard of control of nature, results in subjectivity, envy, and jealousy. The medieval serf had no control over the next plague that would decimate his family, over the meager amount of food he could produce, and over the climactic elements that made his life uncomfortable. He regarded his king as a fabulously wealthy man-god. Yet that same king was less sure of his tomorrows than most people of the modern Western world. Without this sobering comparison to yesteryear, some equate wealth and power. Power does not create or produce. Men who believe that political or dictatorial control over other men will give them control over nature are invited to inhabit some remote jungle and order the construction of cities, the development of medicine, and the production of food. The results would be as bankrupt as their beliefs.

Consider a free, rational society: capitalism. In such a society, each man has access to others' knowledge through the means of free speech. Each man has access (in a specific sense, to be explained) to the property of others. The ability to use all knowledge and all property present in a society magnifies enormously a man's ability to survive. If each man had to discover for himself all medical cures, all engineering feats, and scientific principles, and each man had to build for himself every tool, device, and mechanism, to grow or hunt all his own food and create his own shelter, the length of his life would be brief and its comforts rudimentary. This was the approximate state of affairs during the Dark Ages, a millennium of stagnant existence, the practical outcome of a rigorous application of the ethics of religion. In a free society, all knowledge and all property can be used, according to the right of property ownership, to increase the longevity and standard of living of each man. Instead of redoing and relearning from scratch, man can accumulate knowledge and possessions over time, greatly increasing his ability to survive—i.e., his wealth.

Wealth is the extent of one's ability to survive, specifically a measure of one's ability to command nature to one's own benefit. In society, a man's wealth depends on four factors: his knowledge, his property, the knowledge of others, and the property of others. The effect of the last two factors is in proportion to the degree of freedom in society. For the purposes of this book, we assume a capitalistic society; hence, these two factors are in full effect.

Perhaps the single most important question in economics, is: how can one increase wealth? In the abstract, all one need do is positively affect any one of the four factors listed above. For example, to increase knowledge, economics prescribes scientific research, thereby increasing man's understanding of the world around him and enabling him to make better decisions regarding nature. To increase the value of one's property, economics prescribes productive work, which increases the quantity and quality of such property.

Naturally, these prescriptions apply to every member of society. As we have already seen, the existence of certain freedoms in a society, such as free speech and free trade, positively affect the interaction of these factors amongst members of society.

The right of free speech guarantees that knowledge will grow rather than decay. Moreover, it guarantees access to the knowledge of others. This does not mean one is compelled to share all one's knowledge; only that one cannot be prevented from doing so. Because of language and the written word, knowledge is cumulative. Once an idea is created, it does not disappear, wear out, or become unthought. All the knowledge present in society becomes available for each man to use as he sees fit. Free speech continuously creates wealth.

The right of free trade guarantees access to the property of others, with their consent. Specifically, free trade allows each man to obtain the concretized, tangible knowledge of others. It is enormously easier for one to purchase a computer than to make one oneself. Trade allows producers to specialize their production and consumers to diversify their consumption. This extra degree of freedom (versus producing all one's needs, and consuming only what one produces) results in a tremendous increase in man's wealth. Ongoing trade creates wealth.

Therefore, economics should prescribe freedom of trade in society as a means of increasing wealth. Of particular interest to economic study is the mechanism by which trade increases wealth. As we will see, it is in everyone's direct economic interest to trade. Economists must understand why this is morally right and why it makes practical economic sense.

The morality of free trade is a direct consequence of the right to property. One may dispose of one's property in any manner one chooses. One means of disposal is voluntary, uncoerced trade. Hence, any government interference in trade (which interference by its nature must be coercive) is an attack on one's right to property.

For a discussion of the economic effects of trade, we require several definitions.

A transaction is the voluntary exchange of specified pieces of property or services between two or more specified people at a specified time. Trade is an ongoing sequence of transactions. Free trade is trade not subject to any legal obstructions or conditions. A market is a place, tangible or intangible, where one engages in trade. As a verb, to market means to bring one's goods or services to a market. A market is not a specific set of transactions; transactions occur at a market. The government does not regulate markets, it regulates trade. A regulated market is merely nonsensical; regulated trade is immoral.

Why does the freedom that allows producers to specialize and consumers to diversify, when combined with trade, produce so potent a means of creating wealth? The issue, with reference to controlling nature, is production. The question becomes: why does specialization lead to low-cost production?

Specialization in production enables one to take advantage of economics of scale. In certain cases, it takes less effort per unit produced to produce something, if one produces a large number, than it takes if one produces only one. This principle is called economies of scale. Imagine the effort required for a knowledgeable, isolated individual to produce one color television set from scratch. Undoubtedly, this would represent the effort of a lifetime. Hence, it would not be built—for a single television set is not sufficient production to support an individual for his lifetime, whether he traded it, consumed it, or saved it. Contrast this with the effort required per television set if several men collaborate and undertake to produce one million television sets. Most people would expect the effort per television set to be far less. Why is this so?

Three factors make mass production efficient: capital goods, human specialization, and the principle of division of labor.

Capital goods are machines that produce things. (In accounting, the term capital goods includes all fixed assets and other elements of production, such as raw

materials. This wider meaning is not needed here.)
People do not buy capital goods to consume them; people buy capital goods because they want to make something, possibly even other capital goods. Naturally, it
is much harder to make a machine to make color television sets than it is to make one color television set.
One does not find mass production plants for, say,
Ferraris for this reason. It is not so clear that it is
harder to make a machine to make color television sets
than it is to make one million color television sets
separately, one at a time. Certainly there exists some
number of television sets, a break-even point, at which
one would be better off to produce the capital good first.
Regardless of the number of television sets one wants,
one can always make them individually; there can be
no dis-economies of scale. However, if one wants a
large number of television sets (a great scale of production) one will design a production line. Large-scale production leads to efficiencies not economical with small-
scale production because it allows for the possibility of
capital goods. Hence, the effort expended per unit produced is less.

Human specialization affects the quality and quantity of work an individual can accomplish. Experience
in specific production methods or in specific areas of
technical knowledge enables one to accomplish and
produce more. A commonplace example is the so-called
human learning curve: people spend successively less
time on a repetitive task as they learn from experience,
as can be observed on most automated production
lines. On a less mundane level, imagination and intimate familiarity with a specific production process
may lead one to the knowledge necessary to drastically
improve the process—for example, as Bessemer did
with steel production in the late nineteenth century. In

either case, as in general, specialization results in less effort required per unit produced, a net increase in wealth possible only with trade.

Adam Smith first outlined the principle of division of labor in *The Wealth of Nations*. He used the example of pin production in eighteenth-century Great Britain. Producing one pin requires a number of operations such as drawing the wire, cutting it, straightening it, sharpening the point, etc. One man performing all these tasks spends a great deal of his time proceeding from task to task, setting up to produce, rather than in actual production. If several men share the work (division of labor), far less time is wasted in setup operations or between operations. Hence, less effort is expended per unit produced. This division of labor can be accomplished only if the scale of production is large enough; it is of no value to divide labor to have idle men.

Aside from this technical meaning of division of labor, some writers use the term in the more general sense of specialized production for trade. In contrasting primitive economies in which the family was a self-sufficient economic unit to modern economies in which production is specialized and consumption is diversified, one can say that in the modern economy labor has become divided because the labor required to support a family has been spread across several producers. This characterization describes modern economies, but does not explain their existence. In contrast, the technical meaning provides an economic rationale for mass production—a reason why mass production is efficient.

Because of the possibility of capital goods, the principle of division of labor, and the human learning curve, mass production is more efficient than small-scale production. This efficiency means less effort is required to accomplish other tasks. Hence man's ability to survive (his wealth) is increased. Mass production is possible only if producers specialize. Producers can specialize only if trade is possible. Hence, in a literal and exact sense, trade increases man's wealth. This result is fundamental to all discussion of wealth and trade, and bears repetition. Trade increases wealth by expanding the types of production possible to man.

Any legal restrictions on trade, such as quotas, tariffs, legal monopolies, price controls, or antitrust laws, impair the ability of producers to specialize and hence impose the opportunity cost of lost wealth creation—wealth creation which would have been possible had there been no trade restrictions. This invisible cost is the trade-off to any so-called benefits of trade regulation, moral issues aside. This cost is rarely measured or recognized, being a lost opportunity rather than an immediate, tangible, economic cost, visible to all.

As a concrete example of trade, consider the case of a worker in a factory. A common view is that the factory owner is exploiting the worker, exploitation being meant in a pejorative sense. In reality, both owner and worker are trading economic goods and services. The worker uses the owner's property, the factory, for his own gain—his wages. The owner uses the worker's labor and knowledge for his gain—production for sale and profit. Neither person's gain is possible without the other trading partner. Each is better off than in isolation; wealth has been created.

In a free society the owner is not forced to employ the worker, nor is the worker forced to remain at that particular factory. Each may seek better alternatives. In a totalitarian or semi-free society this freedom may not exist, with a resultant loss in wealth creation.

The owner makes tne investment in a productive asset such as a factory because he expects a return in the form of profit. The consumer of his product also receives a return in the form of better goods or lower prices. A factory will be built, even at enormous cost, if the increased productivity it provides will sufficiently lower the cost of its output, compared to the available alternatives, so as to make the investment an economic one—one that generates profit. Hence investments are undertaken if, a priori, they are expected to create wealth. That is what most do in capitalistic societies.

Wealth is not property. Wealth is not the forcible control of another's will. Wealth is the extent of man's ability to survive. The freedom to think and communicate and the freedom to trade one's property and service are essential to the ongoing creation of wealth.

Chapter Three

Money and Price

More words and less truth are written concerning money than any other subject, save the possible exception of politics. It must rank as the most discussed and least understood topic in all human experience. Though it is pursued relentlessly, few understand its origin, its nature, or the true source of its value. Money is both honored and damned; the love of it has been unjustly blamed for all society's evils since the dawn of recorded history.

The source of this confusion is simple; there has never anywhere appeared an adequate definition of the term money. Attempted definitions have ranged from currency through a medium of exchange to a claim on value. None is a true definition, for a definition must specify a genus (the class of objects to which the defined entity belongs) and a differentia (the characteristic that distinguishes the defined entity from others in the same genus). None of these does so. Nor do they touch on the true nature of money.

The objective of this chapter is an understanding of the nature of money and a concomitant understanding of the price mechanism.

The discussion's context shall be a capitalist society. Free trade and property rights shall exist for all. Protection from violence initiated by others and an objective judicial system shall exist. The effect that the erosion of these freedoms has on the monetary system will be considered at a later time.

Practical experience with money is perhaps as close to the field of economics as a great many individuals come. The ideas presented here are not hard, only different. The only prerequisite is an inquiring mind.

A transaction is a specific exchange in ownership of property between two specific individuals at a specific time. A system of trade in which all transactions consist of the direct exchange of goods or services is called a barter system. In primitive societies, barter was and is the dominant form of trade. As society becomes more sophisticated and complex, barter becomes unwieldy.

Consider two individuals, A possessing guns and desiring butter, and B possessing butter and desiring guns. A transaction seems the obvious answer. Note that the terms buyer and seller are inappropriate in this case; the roles are symmetrical. The important question is: what are the necessary conditions that enable the transaction to take place?

First, A and B must find each other. In small societies this is not a serious problem, but as the range of goods and services and the number of people increase this difficulty can create a serious impediment to trade. Imagine an individual living in New York City who wants to trade a portion of his output as a securities analyst for a size 9, extra wide, black leather, wingtip shoe. Finding his counterpart with the shoes and in need of securities analysis in a city of millions would take some detective work. Matching up complementary traders may take a large, real expenditure of time and effort. If this expenditure is not warranted by the benefits derived from the trade, trade would cease.

Second, traders face a temporal problem. A trader's counterpart may not exist at the specific moment of time he wants to make his trade. In our example here, it may be the case that all shoe owners are looking for food, not securities analysis. Hence, A must either wait or work through a third party, someone who will accept securities analysis in exchange for food, so that he may then approach the shoe owners.

Barter has two difficulties. First, one must locate potential trading partners, individuals with highly specific needs. This difficulty increases in proportion to the size and complexity of the society. Second, a more fundamental problem, transactions must occur at a specific point in time, and there is no guarantee that the appropriate trading partner will exist.

These problems are serious impediments to trade. Because trade increases wealth, and because wealth is a universally desired end, methods were developed to circumvent these difficulties.

Some progress can be made within a pure barter

economy. One improvement occurs if individuals specialize in the business of trading.

The original middleman was the bright soul who acquired a large inventory of tradeable goods and offered to trade with all who would meet his terms. Because the goods were not for his personal use, he would trade with anyone who offered a suitable deal. He did not suffer the constraints of someone trading for his own account. A new trading flexibility appeared. The goods that a middleman possesses are not for his personal consumption, but for the express purpose of trade—therefore, he can take trade advantage of other traders' differing requirements, the fact that specific goods have different values to different traders at different times. The middleman achieves the separation of traders by splitting the original transaction (which now never occurs) in half and positioning himself in the middle. Instead of dealing with each other, both traders deal with the middleman. The traders do not have to worry about finding each other or even if their counterpart exists. The original transaction is split in half and replaced with two transactions which are independent in space and time. Middlemen vastly increase the ability of society to trade by allowing traders to operate independently. Middlemen exist because the real cost of supporting them is less than the real cost incurred by traders trying to find each other without assistance. Middlemen support themselves by buying low and selling high. Low and high are relative terms, and the trader finds the middleman's idea of high lower than locating a trading partner himself. Otherwise he would not use the middleman. Yet middlemen do exist, so obviously someone finds it economic to use them.

The middleman splits the original intended trans-

action into two independent, separate transactions. He
does so in the clumsiest, crudest, most inelegant way—
he inserts himself into both halves of the transaction.
Instead of A's guns for B's butter, we have A's guns for
M's butter, and M's guns for B's butter. Does it not seem
likely a more efficient solution is possible? Why go to
the trouble of warehousing guns and butter and the
expense of supporting the middleman's existence?

In place of a middleman, can one substitute a universal trading commodity (UTC)? Using it, A would trade
(sell) his guns for some of C's UTC and then trade (buy)
some of D's butter for this same UTC. As when the
middleman is involved, B, the ideal trading partner
with butter and in need of guns, need not exist. This
UTC cannot be something of intrinsic economic value
that one wishes to have for its own sake (like guns or
butter); rather it is something used exclusively to facilitate trading. It must have generalized value.

If in trying to trade guns for butter, A discovers B
wants to trade clothes for butter, A can do one of two
things. One, he can try to locate C, who wants to trade
guns for clothes, a duplication of his original problem.
Two, he can introduce this UTC and split his transaction in two as above, avoiding the necessity of dealing
with a middleman.

What is this UTC? How much is "some" of it? In
splitting his transaction in half (that is, alleviating
himself of the need to deal with or indeed even find B),
A is faced with two large problems. How is he to value
this UTC and how much should he get for his guns?
How can he convince a third party possessing butter
that this UTC has value?

When A dealt directly with B, the method by which A
valued the transaction was clear. Both A and B agreed
that so much butter was worth so many guns, or else no

transaction occurred. With the transaction split, A no longer has this luxury. Instead of a specific claim on certain of B's property, he is left with a general claim on some unspecified persons' unspecified property at some unspecified point in time. How can this claim be measured? How can its value be made *objectively verifiable*?

In order to quantify the size of a transaction, one needs a scale of measurement. A measurement[1] is the identification of a quantitative relationship by means of a standard that serves as a unit. The standard must be immutable and absolute. When using a middleman, no scale is needed. He can match the value across both transactions subjectively because he is still dealing within a barter system. Splitting the transaction via a universal commodity requires an objective scale of measurement. What is the appropriate scale? One does not measure distance in pounds. With what unit does one measure economic value? How is a particular measurement made?

This line of reasoning leads, of course, to the concepts of money and price. The UTC is money. The appropriate unit is the dollar. A particular measurement corresponds to a price. However, giving correct names to these concepts is not the same as defining them or showing how they operate.

How can an individual measure the worth of an object he possesses or wants to possess through trade? More generally, how can he compare the values of different objects? How can a trader make this measurement objective and therefore acceptable to other traders?

In the sample transaction of A's guns for B's UTC, A gave up and B received some guns. What is the worth of

---

[1]   A. Rand, op. cit., p. 8.

that to each? More important, what is the source of worth?

A and B live in a finite world and must deal with the limitations of doing so. Neither has infinite resources. A cannot have everything he perceives that is of economic or other value. There is a limit to the property he possesses, to the property that others possess, and to the property that exists. When A gives up some of his guns, the loss of value occurs because he has given up some part of his total possessions, and his possessions are part of his means of survival.[2] What part has he forsaken?

Because his possessions are not necessarily homogeneous and because his determination of value is done with reference to himself (a personal value assessment), there is no natural unit for value. One cannot meaningfully say, "This object is worth 9 utils," in the sense that a util would mean the same thing to both A and B. The only way A can determine his loss is to compare the forsaken object to the others he still possesses. A can meaningfully say, "Object 1 is worth twice object 2," or equivalently, "I would substitute object 1 for two of object 2, and vice versa." In this way he can compare the relative worths of all his possessions.

This does not mean that A's assessments are in some way the "right" ones or "objectively meaningful for B." The more rational and intelligent A is, the more closely correlated his assessments will be with the objects' use in increasing the quality and quantity of his life.

Hence, A can value his possessions in a proportional manner (object 1 is worth twice object 2, object 2 is worth five times object 3, etc.) by considering various

---

[2]   An interesting analogy is the finiteness of man's lifetime; time becomes the currency of his life, for him to spend as he wills.

substitutions amongst the objects.[3] If A possesses four objects with relative worths of 1, 4, 9, and 36, it is clear that object 2 represents 4/(1+4+9+36) or 8% of A's possessions. By comparing the proportional measure to the total, the constant of proportionality drops out and one is left with an objective measurement of the relative worth of each object to A at that time.

Analogously, a group of traders can compare their general claims (quantities of UTC) only by relating their individual claims to the total claim. This is possible only if the total claim is an agreed-upon amount. Then each trader's claim becomes a fraction of the total and his holding of UTC represents that claim. In this case there is an objective unit as defined below. Therefore the total amount of UTC must be fixed. (Note that we have not addressed the question: given an agreed-upon total claim, how is this claim distributed amongst traders? This is equivalent to: how can a society convert from a barter economy to a monetary economy? Since we already live in a monetary economy, the question is of only historical interest.)

In practice, a suitable physical commodity is chosen as the UTC and a specified amount of it is set equal to one unit (e.g., 1/35th ounce of gold = $1). Because the total amount of gold present in the world is (approximately) fixed, there is a number that represents the total number of UTC units (35 times the number of ounces of gold present) in circulation. A given individual can own a certain amount of gold which he can use as UTC to transact directly for the goods and services he desires. He knows the value of any given amount of gold (as money) because he knows the total amount of gold and the portion thereof his represents. In practice,

---

[3] For a discussion of the technical issues involved in this evaluation, see the appendix, which can be omitted on a first reading.

he may not be aware of the total amount of gold, so he uses transactions similar to the ones he is contemplating as a benchmark; that is, he observes the going price.

Note the important distinction between this case and the example in which a single individual evaluates the worth of his possessions. One individual assigned values from a fixed total to all his objects and then transformed his measurements via proportionality so that the total was, say, 1. There is no need for a UTC. In the case of many individuals, the overall sum of measurements is fixed and this sum is represented by a fixed amount of UTC, which is then used to allocate the various subsums to individuals. Any given individual's sum is not fixed; the total of all individuals is. Because of trade, the amount of gold an individual owns, if gold is the UTC, is variable. One's gold represents a general claim on others' possessions—an objective claim since that gold represents x% of the total gold in circulation as a UTC. People cooperate with this general claim because it is in their interest to do so. The mechanism of a UTC vastly facilitates trade and hence increases wealth. The fact that the total quantity of gold is fixed insures that the these claims will have an objectively verifiable value.

This system does not require all existing objects to have a monetary value assigned to them nor does it mean that the total amount of money represents the total wealth of society. Instead, money serves two functions. First, it defines a scale of measurement so that the size of a transaction can be objectively verifiable. Second, it allocates (by means of physical possession) the general claims of traders on other, unspecified traders; i.e., it fixes those claims so they do not become subjective, unmeasurable, or never-ending. Thus money can store wealth and provide a means of exchange.

Because of this, money does much more than merely increase the efficiency of barter. By providing a scale of measurement, money allows economic calculation—that is, a means to decide whether some given complex system of production is efficient (relatively good vis-a-vis other methods), whether it will produce a profit. Without money, complex methods of production are incapable of evaluation. Money allows a society to vastly increase the scope of production and trade, and therefore wealth.

Money, therefore, is any fungible physical commodity with the following characteristics, and used in the following way. An arbitrary but fixed physical amount (i.e., weight) of this commodity is assigned the value of one unit. The total amount of the physical commodity used as money must be fixed at "n" units, "n" normally being a large number. This commodity must be such that it is possible to identify and designate which portion is being used as money and which portion is not being used that way. This commodity, for reasons to be made clear, must have no intrinsic economic usefulness; that is, its use stems only from its use as money, not from any other use. This commodity is then used as an objective scale of measurement to value transactions. Moreover, the amount of this commodity in anyone's physical possession serves to measure and account for (make concrete) the size of that person's general claim on other traders, exercised through the use of this commodity as a UTC in trade. The purpose of money is to measure objectively and account for each individual's general claim on other traders.

A price is a measurement of the size of a particular transaction according to the scale derived by using the money unit defined in the previous paragraph as a standard. Note that price is an historic measure of one particular transaction; it measures the size of a change in ownership of a specific piece of property from one specified person to another at a specific point in time.

A monetary transaction is a transaction in which one trading party (the buyer) pays money to the other trading party (the seller), who provides a good or service.

The money unit chosen is arbitrary. The only consideration in determining its size should be to make the numbers associated with normal-sized transactions "human-sized." The most natural scale would be to fix the total amount of money at 1 (unit) and work in fractions, emphasizing the nature of the money mechanism. However, because modern society is made of hundreds of millions of people, each making many transactions daily, the use of this scale would put most transactions on the order of a billionth of a money unit, hardly a human-sized number or one easy to work with. Hence, it is easier to scale everything up by a factor of, say, a billion. The resulting unit is a dollar. The problem with this approach is that one loses sight of the total, in this case one billion. This has had disastrous consequences.

The presently available forms of money suffer from two defects. One, the physical good chosen can generally be produced independently. This destroys its value as money, for any scale of measurement must be fixed and objective. Production of the chosen physical good would destroy the certainty, the information, the good is supposed to represent, rendering it useless. Two, any physical good chosen may have its own intrinsic economic usefulness. It may be desired for itself more than for its role as money. If this occurs, the physical good becomes part of the barter system (that is, a particular commodity versus a universal commodity) and the benefits of a monetary system are lost. The money, the information represented by the physical commodity, disappears.

Gold has been used as money for centuries. Many people regard gold as the only true money man has invented, but it is only one of many possible moneys. It is imperfect, first used because it was the best available. Gold suffers from both problems mentioned in the previous paragraph. The amount of gold in circulation is not fixed, nor even predictable. Anyone could discover a gold mine and increase the quantity of gold. This would reduce its value to man, both as an economic good and as money. Specifically, it would reduce the real wealth of those who choose to hold gold rather than other assets such as land, by reducing the objective value of the general claim on other traders that the gold represents. There would be a greater quantity of gold available to trade for real assets so the owners of gold would have their claim reduced. Also, gold has direct economic uses which interfere with its role as money. People desire gold for reasons quite apart from its value as money. Ancients prized gold for jewelry and ornamentation; modern man uses gold in industry—for example, in electronics manufacturing. This dual role frustrates the use of gold as money. It is possible non-monetary uses of gold would use of the bulk of available gold, leaving a small and variable amount to serve the monetary system.

These two problems cause the same difficulty. They change the total amount of gold used as money, thereby invalidating the size of the claims represented by gold, destroying the objectivity of the money system.

Man subsequently developed an improved form of money as a replacement for gold. The improvement resulted because the new form had no intrinsic economic value, although this is not widely understood. It is the dominant form of money in circulation today: paper money. One does not find any pure silver coin in circulation today; people found its economic value as silver to be higher than its nominal value as money. Paper money does not suffer from this problem. One can hold paper money as a means to an end, but in and of itself it is worthless. Unfortunately, paper money suffers a fatal flaw. Its management is left in the hands of the government. Its value is destroyed by increasing its quantity for political reasons. This quantity is not fixed, nor even predictable. The information and objectivity it represents is destroyed by an influx of paper. Governments, operating through central banks, have demonstrated no ability to responsibly manage this form of money. Governments moved money from the realm of economics to the realm of politics. Governments that practice this destruction of money suffer from self-delusion if they feel secure that their actions go unnoticed. A measure of people's willingness to hold paper money, and hence their opinion of its value, can be obtained by observing how much of it they are willing to trade for gold, a substance only marginally more useful than paper. The paper prices paid for gold are a direct indication of people's trust in their government's monetary integrity.

A monetary system which suffers from neither of these problems, and hence is an improvement over all existing systems, is adumbrated in a later chapter.

Because money provides an objective scale of measurement, all monetary transactions have an associated particular measurement—the price of the transaction. The price measures the economic size of the transaction. It is an objective measurement of the economic size of a transaction. Recall that a transaction is the exchange in ownership of two specific pieces of property between two specified individuals at a specified juncture.

The nature of money illuminates the most horrendous practical problem of socialism—economic calculation. The very existence of money depends on the existence of voluntary, uncoerced transactions amongst traders. Without such voluntary action price is meaningless, no economic calculation is possible, and there is no way to judge the economic efficacy of various production methods. Therefore, socialism must necessarily provide a greatly reduced standard of living—it is, in fact, a barter system. On a less grandiose scale, we see that so-called price controls are merely an attempt to destroy the economic significance of money, resulting in irrational trading behavior and a reduced standard of living.

The primary issue regarding prices is: what determines price? That is, what determines the size of a particular transaction? How do the two participants in a transaction come to agree on the appropriate price?

Before one can answer this question, one must note the following important distinction. A price refers to the size of a particular transaction. A price does not refer to the goods involved in the transaction. A commodity does not have a price as an attribute; rather, if a commodity is involved in a transaction, a price is determined and measures the size of the transaction, not the commodity. To have a price, one needs a buyer, a seller, a juncture, and a commodity—not merely the commodity. People speak of the price of a good; they are in fact referring to the prices of recent transactions involving that good. Similarly, one speaks of an object as priceless; one means that neither that object nor one similar has been traded before in one's experience (not that its value is infinite). It is entirely possible for two

individuals to pay different amounts for the same
object, or that one individual will pay different amounts
for the same object at different times.

In everyday usage, gold and numerous other commodities such as metals, stocks, bonds, agricultural
products, and raw materials are assigned a "price."
This occurs because the markets for these items are
large and liquid, so the numerous transactions occurring do so at approximately the same price over short
periods of time. Traders would object to large differences and in fact would arbitrage across these differences. However, even in these markets, there are small
variations. The daily London, Zurich, and New York
fixing for the "price" of gold are rarely identical, for the
simple reason that, to a trader, gold in Zurich is not
identical to gold in New York; it is a different location.
The over-the-counter stock market quotes bid and
asked prices for each security, merely listing the most
recent offers.

A price is assigned to transactions, not commodities.
A monetary transaction consists of four things: a
buyer, a seller, a juncture, and a good or service. Therefore, to understand how prices are determined, one
should concentrate on understanding the dynamics of
transactions—that is, trading—rather than attempt-
ing some "objective" assessment of what some particular good or service is worth. The latter is not a fixed
number. One cannot measure value outside the context
of human survival. The best one could do is quote what
oneself would pay for the good at present, hardly a
generalized model of price determination.

In any given potential monetary transaction, both
the buyer and the seller have two decisions to make.
One must decide what one wants to buy (sell). One must
decide what price one is willing to pay (accept). The

second decision forces the buyer (seller) to make objective the worth he places on the object to be procured (sold). The only way a person can do this is to compare the object to others that would achieve his desired goal—that is, to compare the value of that alternative to others he could pursue.

The source of measurement of worth is the decision-making ability of the trader in the context of a finite world—his ability to create and evaluate alternative courses of action that attain his objective. In economic, as opposed to metaphysical, terms this means the economic value one places on an object as a buyer (seller) is determined by what alternative products one could buy (sell) and by what alternative markets one could trade in.

These alternative transactions are a benchmark that allows one to peg the value of an object based on previous trading experience. If the object is commonplace, there will be a fairly small variation in the price agreed to by different sets of traders. In cases of unusual or unique objects, people have less experience to draw on, and hence do a less consistent job of pricing.

An example of the latter is the sale of a business enterprise—a large and complex entity that will not have been previously sold in anything like its present form. In such cases, there are often wide variations in the bid prices of different potential buyers.

If one took a strictly barter economy and introduced the money mechanism to traders with no previous experience of it, one would initially find large variations in the prices paid for transactions involving similar goods. As people developed experience in monetary transactions, these variations would decrease, but not disappear.

Usually, there exist alternatives and options for both

buyer and seller, even if only the choice not to buy (sell).
These include: a different buyer (seller), a different
commodity, or a different juncture. Each alternative
must be evaluated by each trader with his own personal value assessment before a decision is made, a
price determined, and a transaction enacted. If buyer
and seller cannot reach an agreement, no transaction
is made and no price determined. The buyer's alternatives form an upper limit to the price of a transaction,
and the seller's a lower limit. If these overlap, a transaction will be made at some intermediate price. Each
trader must understand the opportunity cost of a
transaction—the value of various options no longer
available after a given transaction is made.

Traders must agree on price because this is the
method by which the money mechanism makes objective, and therefore amendable to agreement, the claims
represented by each trader's money. With no price,
there can be no monetary transaction.

A transaction consists of the exchange of ownership
of two specified pieces of property by two specified
traders at a specified time. A monetary transaction is a
transaction in which one of the pieces of property is
money. All monetary transactions have an associated
price, the amount of money involved, which measures
the size of the transaction. Prices are determined by the
alternatives available to both buyer and seller, and
their respective evaluations of same. Money provides a
means to transform the generalized trading claims
into an objective scale of measurement and so provide
a price.

The foregoing is a description of the nature of prices
and the factors involved in determining a particular
price. It is not to be construed as a means to predict
prices; to do so would require a full understanding of

the values and abilities of the individuals involved, as well as an enumeration of all possessions of each trader, a task outside the abilities of present-day science.

Nonetheless, this description is useful. Its first use will be to refute the false macroeconomic policy practiced by today's economists and politicians.

The concepts of "supply" and "demand" play no direct role in this model of price determination. Price models dependent on supply and demand ignore the fundamental observations that a price can be ascribed only to a transaction, not to a good, and that all prices are decided individually, by individuals, not by some macroeconomic collective consisting of intersecting supply and demand curves.

The spurious assignment of prices to goods rather than transactions leads to another serious difficulty. It becomes natural to inquire about the relationship of the "price" of a good to time. Because any transaction is fixed in time, this issue does not arise if one uses prices correctly. This nonexistent relationship has led to incredibly bad management of the monetary system through the confusion of monetary and pricing phenomena.

One sees how the inadequacies of barter led naturally to the development of money. A second offshoot of barter's shortcomings is explored in the next chapter.

Chapter Four

Credit

The previous chapter introduced money as a mechanism which facilitated trade by overcoming certain inadequacies of pure barter and, in so doing, greatly increased the rate of creation of wealth. This chapter introduces another mechanism, the credit mechanism, which overcomes barter's inadequacies in a different manner. Combining these two mechanisms forms an exceptionally potent tool to encourage trade, one that provides the basis of most modern trade.

The concept of money resulted from considering ways to split a given transaction. Specifically, it split apart the traders involved in a transaction, alleviating their necessity of dealing with each other. The concept of credit also results from considering ways to split a given transaction; however, it is not the traders that are split apart. Instead, one splits the exchange of property ownership across time; ownership of one piece of property changes now, and ownership of the other changes later. The device used to effect this is a promise to pay. Money overcomes primarily the physical problems of barter; credit overcomes the temporal ones.

If A, as a producer of butter, can anticipate his need of guns, the following avenue is open to him in the case he finds that B, the weapons producer, has no guns at the time A has butter. A can give up his butter to B on the understanding that, when B produces guns at some later date, he owes them to A. Instead of trading the ownership of tangible commodities, A gives up his goods for a promise, a promise to pay. That promise is a promise of future action on B's part. That action is the willful transfer of ownership of certain guns to A. The middleman's function of splitting the transaction is again achieved, without use of a middleman. However, it is not traders A and B that are split apart. Instead, the introduction of an intangible promise to pay enables the timing of change of ownership to be split: B receives his butter now, A will receive his guns later.

Alternatively, one can regard the promise to pay as barterable commodity and conclude that A traded tangible goods for an intangible commodity—a promise. Effectively, B has sold a future action on his part. Hence, credit implies the existence of risk—the risk of non-repayment. This risk will vary depending on the honorability of the individual extending the promise, but it will never vanish; the promise is made by an individual and an individual's actions are never one hundred percent predictable, even by himself. In credit transactions, one trader gives up something tangible (some fraction of his property) for a promise that may never be honored. He assumes credit risk, the risk of non-repayment. He does so because his incentive to trade is wealth and he is compensated for undertaking risk through the mechanism of price—a process to be discussed.

Note the uncertain value of this type of transaction prior to final redemption of the promise to pay. Its value is dependent on B's honoring his promise and A's acceptance of this promise. A may find the promise he holds to be an unmarketable commodity of uncertain value. His assessment of B's credit risk may be different from that of other people.

Therefore, a credit transaction is a transaction in which the change of ownership of goods between the two parties involved is not simultaneous. Credit is the promise to pay one trader accepts in lieu of immediate payment. Credit implies the existence of credit risk—the risk of non-repayment. Instead of receiving B's goods immediately, A receives a promise to pay to be honored at some specified future date. A holds credit rather than goods or money. Because of the credit risk involved in B's promise, the value to A of the transaction is less than A's estimate of the value of the goods to be turned over to A. It is less by a factor that accounts for the likelihood of repayment and by a factor that accounts for the lack of opportunity to use these goods for a certain time. This likelihood diminishes as the specified time for payment extends into the future. A promise of payment tomorrow is more likely to be honored than a promise of payment next year.

A credit transaction, and hence credit, can be created in any amount at will by any two traders, independently of any other traders' actions. This attribute of credit is important for a comparison of credit and money.

Credit is a very general concept; concrete examples exhibit an exceptionally wide range of characteristics. Its form is limited only by the ingenuity of the traders involved.

The most rudimentary form of credit transaction is that in which payment is simply delayed by one trading party with the consent of the other. Most business-to-business transactions are of this form. Goods and services are not actually paid for until, say, thirty days after receipt. When A transfers ownership of certain goods to B, all he gets in return is B's promise (usually legally binding, but that is irrelevant in the context of economics) to provide payment within a short time period. Hence, the mechanism of a promise to pay enables the traders to split the transaction by allowing non-simultaneous transfer of ownership. If B's situation should change for the worse in the interim, A may be out of luck. Although the motivation for credit here is normally simple convenience and efficiency, in some cases this credit may provide a significant portion of B's financing.

A more involved form of credit is the promissory note: a formal, legal agreement between two parties involving the transfer of funds from one to the other and the return of those funds and more at some specified later time. The "and more" is the first trader's return for extending credit risk. The second trader is willing to pay this "and more" because the immediate use of the funds allows him to do something he would otherwise be unable to do—usually an investment of some kind which will hopefully create the wealth needed to repay the "and more," and more.

With more than two traders, things become more complicated. For example, consider an ordinary check. In accepting a check for payment, A is extending credit to B, the issuer of the check, for B may not have the funds in his account to cover the check. Moreover, A is also extending credit to the bank named on the check. It is possible, although in practice extremely unlikely, that the bank may go bankrupt before A cashes B's check, even though B had sufficient funds in his account to cover the check. This can occur because B has in turn extended credit to the bank in the form of a bank account or demand deposit.

In well-developed markets, credit may be packaged in sophisticated ways to increase its marketability. A company can sell convertible bonds—ordinary bonds (that is, promissory notes with periodic interest payments) with various but specific rights or privileges attached. Under certain conditions these bonds are convertible into shares of common equity, allowing the purchaser to own directly a piece of the company, with the possibility of significant capital gain. These or other rights affect the value and marketability of these bonds. Other more complicated instruments are marketed today as investors become more sophisticated and the tax law grows more complex.

Opening a bank account is a credit transaction. Except for safe-deposit boxes, banks do not provide mere physical security for property. Banks provide a promise to pay, usually on demand, in return for money. Again, various privileges can be attached to this form of credit, and hence affect its price. These include: the right to issue checks against the balance, the right to preferred loan rates, the right to monthly statements, and even the right to (admittedly somewhat biased) financial or investment advice. The bank offers these services to attract the funds it needs for its investment program.

Insurance is also a form of credit transaction. Money buys a promise to pay. In the case of insurance, this promise is honored only under certain specified conditions such as death, accident, or fire. For this reason the price people pay is far less than for a corresponding unconditional promise to pay. Insurance is used to provide protection against catastrophes—disastrous events with a very small chance of occurrence.

While not an exhaustive summary, the foregoing examples indicate the variety possible in credit transactions. Credit exists solely because of its ability to facilitate trade, to make trade possible in circumstances it otherwise would not be, and thereby to increase man's ability to create wealth. Credit transactions occur, as do all transactions, only if both parties believe that they will be better off after making the transaction. Man's reason insures this is usually the case.

In a modern economy, practically all credit transactions involve money; the promise to pay is a promise to pay money. These credit transactions are called monetary credit transactions. In addition, it may be the case that the commodity offered on credit is money itself. This form of credit, called financial credit, in which money is lent and repaid has been the source of an enormous confusion between money and credit, one that will be clarified presently.

Financial credit transactions have a price because the lender buys a promise to pay with money. The simplest form of financial credit is the promissory note. If A, in assessing the risks of non-repayment in B's request for money, decides that he will offer $80 for B's promise to pay $100 in a year's time, A is valuing B's promise at $80. If B accepts this deal, the price of his promise is established at $80. The monetary value (economic size) of B's offer to pay $100 in one year is $80. Hence the price paid for B's promissory note is $80. If B's promise to pay were due at a different time, say in two years, the price of the promise would be different—say, $64.[1] This reduction in price occurs because the risk of non-payment on B's part increases over time and because A will be without his money for a longer period. (In today's world, it also occurs because the scale of measurement provided by money is not constant over time as a result of incorrect government policy; this distinct cause is explored in the next chapter.) Hence, the decreasing value of B's promise as it extends over time measures the rate at which the risk of non-payment is incurred if one extends credit over time to B. The fundamental link between time and value leads to a method of measuring directly the rate at which risk is incurred.

In the example above, A paid $80 for B's promise to pay $100 in one year. The ratio of these numbers measures the riskiness of the credit extended—namely, 100/80 or 1.25. One would conclude that a transaction with a ratio of 1.5 over the same time period has a higher estimate of risk of non-payment. Because we are measuring a rate, there must be a standard time period, usually one year. Hence, in this example the measure of credit risk is, more correctly, 1.25 per year. This is not the price of the transaction; that was, is, and always will be $80.

Because, perhaps, of the immediacy of the act, most individuals in this situation focus on the $80 paid to B, rather than the $100 B promises to pay to A. From this

---

[1]   For reasons which will become clear.

perspective, A lends B $80, and B must repay the $80 along with a premium of $20 to compensate A for the risk he has undertaken. A's focus is the $20 he hopes to gain for risking $80. The ratio of this premium (as opposed to the amount to be repaid) with the price of the transaction gives 20/80 or .25, a number 1 less than that calculated above. In normal circumstances, this ratio will be less than 1, and so is expressed as a percentage, 25% per year. In this form it is called an interest rate.

Viewing the transaction as the sale of a promise to pay, A brought B's promise to pay $100 in one year for $80 and so evaluated his credit risk at 1.25 per year. Viewing the transaction as B borrowing $80 from A results in an interest rate of 25% per year, which reflects the credit risk A has assumed. Hence, we see the reason for valuing B's promise to pay $100 in two years at $64: $100/1.25/1.25 = $64. These two viewpoints are equally valid, but the latter, that of B borrowing from A, is more common. Regardless of one's perspective, the underlying reality remains unchanged.

In summary, financial credit transactions have an associated price. Because most financial credit transactions are of certain standard forms, in common usage one transforms the price into a rate using a ratio over a standard time period. Expressed as a percentage, this rate is called an interest rate. From it, one can compute the future or present value of a promise, and one can assess the credit risk inherent in a given financial credit transaction. There exists a whole arithmetic science and nomenclature associated with interest rates on which any introductory text on finance will elaborate.

Exactly speaking, the price of a financial credit transaction is the money paid for the promise to pay. In informal usage, one speaks less accurately of an interest rate as being the "price of credit." Not only does credit not have a price (transactions do, and only if they involve money), the interest rate is a transformation of the price of a specific transaction, not the price itself. However, this usage is probably too widespread to combat successfully. No distinction is made between interest rates and prices, nor between credit in general and financial credit transactions. Limited to this, the confusion is not too harmful. When combined with a confusion between credit and money, it leads to an atrocity called "the price of money." Money does not have a price; money is used to measure prices, including the prices of financial credit transactions. Inquiring as to the price of money is analogous to questioning the length of distance itself or the age of time itself.

Combining credit and money forms a powerful tool of trade ideally suited to efficient trading. Financial credit efficiently allocates resources to various investments by comparing their relative risks. The confusion between money and credit requires that one take a closer look at their similarities and differences.

Both credit and money are mechanisms that enable one to split apart pure barter transactions and greatly increase the efficiency of trade. Money splits transactions across traders; credit splits transactions across time. The similarity ends here.

Money exists in a fixed amount, so as to provide an objective, invariant scale of measurement. Credit can be created at will, independently by any two traders at any time.

One undertakes no credit risk in holding money. Its claim is objectively verifiable and universally good. One incurs credit risk in holding credit, the risk of non-payment.

Financial credit transactions have an associated

price. The price is often stated as an interest rate, which measures the rate at which risk is incurred. This risk is determined interactively—the two traders estimate and agree upon a rate. Money has no price—it provides the scale by which prices are set.

Ownership of money is always transferable, for its value is set objectively. Credit is not necessarily transferable at any price, let alone the price paid for it.

One realizes a return on holding money because a general claim on wealth, objectively measured, will increase in value over time in a capitalistic society. This results from the fact that it represents a constant fraction of total wealth, and total wealth is increasing due to production allowed by trade. One also realizes a return in holding credit; however, its a priori expected increase in value must be greater than that expected from holding money. After all, one expects to be compensated for incurring risk. Otherwise one would not incur it.

A promise to pay, the ultimate value of which is contingent on the future actions of a specific individual, is not the same as a general claim on wealth, the value of which is objectively verifiable. Money is not credit.

However, money is greatly confused with credit. Because there exists an amount of money—the number of dollars of currency in circulation—economists who do not distinguish money and credit proceed to calculate the value of all credit outstanding in the economy. Changes in its value over time cause great concern in financial markets. Economists ignore that any two individuals can change its value independently at any time. The sum so computed has no more significance than, say, the sum of prices of all transactions involving automobiles occurring in the last six months.

Imagine two small, distinct societies each with $1,000

of currency in circulation. In society A credit is non-existent, and all transactions are either barter or monetary. In society B an individual C sells promises to pay for an amount totaling $1,000 and destroys all the currency he received for these promises. A monetarist economist would claim the total amount of "money" (his name for money plus credit) is identical in both cases, $1,000. However, in society A trading would continue uninterrupted. In B, monetary trade would disintegrate as C's promises came due—for there is no money with which to pay as promised! Worse, there is no longer any money with which to value those promises—no scale of measurement exists. A specific promise to pay $100 is not honorable—the currency required to pay it does not exist. This promise is not even capable of being valued; the mechanism to set prices has been destroyed. To argue that one could pay off this promise with another promise merely postpones the day of reckoning, and ignores the question: how does one value this new promise? In truth, it is value-less.

Two societies, each with a constant and equal amount of "money plus credit," reach markedly different ends. Hence, the monetarist's claim that money is currency plus credit is false, as is his claim that credit is money or that interest rates are prices.[2]

Money is any fungible physical commodity with the following characteristics and used in the following way. An arbitrary but fixed physical amount (weight) of this commodity is assigned the value of one unit. The total amount of this commodity is fixed at "n" units

---

[2] This example points out the inappropriateness of the term "money supply." Its use suggests that the "amount of money" can and should be varied. Observing the distinction between money and credit eliminates the confusion.

("n" usually being a large number). The commodity must have no intrinsic economic usefulness. The value stems only from its role as money, not from any other use. This commodity is then used as an objective scale of measurement to value transactions. Moreover, the amount of this commodity in one's physical possession serves to measure and account for (make concrete) the size of that person's general claim on other traders, obtained through the use of this commodity as a universal trading commodity.

Money has neither a price nor an interest rate.

Credit is a promise to pay on the part of one trader to another. The promisee holds the promise to pay in lieu of the object promised. He extends credit to the promisor. A credit transaction is one involving credit—that is, involving a promise to pay. A financial credit transaction is a credit transaction in which one trader buys a promise to pay with money, and so puts a price on the credit transaction. The object being promised usually is, but need not be, money. The price of a financial credit transaction is the amount of money paid for the promise. An interest rate is a measurement of the risk of non-payment incurred, expressed as a percentage per year, calculated by dividing the amount of premium required per year by the price of the financial credit transaction.

Chapter Five

Inflation

The definition of money requires that the total quantity of currency be fixed to preserve the objectivity of the claims represented by money. We wish to consider the effects of loosening this restriction.

Because a price is transaction specific (it measures the size of a monetary transaction according to a given scale), we must find a way to compare measurements of a particular transaction using currencies which are managed differently.

To do this, we take a fully capitalistic society and

give it four currencies (A, B, C, and D), each of which will be handled differently. Each is legal tender and can be used in monetary trade.

Currency A exists in a fixed amount. It corresponds exactly to the definition of money. The other currencies are increased in quantity each year by different methods. At the end of each year, anyone holding currency B is given an additional amount of newly created currency B equal to 5% of his current holdings. The total amount of currency C is also increased by 5%, but the government owns the whole of this increase. The increase in currency D is also given to the government, but its amount is not predetermined. A toss of a fair coin at year-end determines whether the increase shall be 5% or 25%.

We wish to compare the nature of the general claim on wealth represented by the different currencies, the size of specific claims, and the beneficiaries of these claims.

Currency A is the control currency; we take the prices it defines as standard, because the unit standard defined by it is constant.

Currency B will be identical with currency A until the end of year one. At that time, each individual owning currency B increases his nominal currency B moneyholding by 5%, and simultaneously the unit standard defined by currency B decreases by a factor $1/1.05$, because the overall number of money units is increased by a factor of 1.05.

Two observations merit notice. First, the currency B owners have not been changed. There are no new owners (5% of nothing is nothing) and there are no previous owners who are now not owners (5% of something is something). Second, the size of these claims remains unchanged. Because the money mechanism works proportionally, the size of a claim is invariant under the transformation made. Each currency B holder owns more units but there are just as many more units overall. The relevant measure is the size of each holder's holdings divided by the total money in circulation. If an individual holding currency B owns N units and the total in circulation is M, the size of his claim on wealth is N/M. After the year-end increase, an individual holding currency B will now own 1.05N units, but the total in circulation is now 1.05M, so the size of his claim is 1.05N/1.05M which equals N/M.

All that has changed is the unit scale of measurement. A society could certainly change the length of distance represented by a foot so that it is smaller by 5% each year. This is a change of scale. It does not affect the actual size of any distance, only which number is used to represent that size. Similarly, the change in monetary unit described does not change the actual size of any transaction—only the number used to represent that size, the price. This is the same as converting from feet to inches.

Therefore, the price paid for an item, if paid in currency B, will be greater than if paid in currency A. It will be 5% higher for every year the experiment has been in progress—but it will represent the same size claim under either currency (as it must; we are considering the same transaction). The increase reflects only a change in scale of measurement.

Because of the proportional nature of measurement by money, a pre-announced change in the unit standard of measurement of money does not affect trading patterns—specifically, which transactions occur—but does affect the associated prices. More exactly, an increase in money units of x% (that is, a decrease in the monetary unit of 1/[1+x%]) will increase the price measurement of a specific transaction by x% over what it would have been had there been no increase.

With currency C, the situation is different. Not only is the unit scale of measurement changed annually, new owners are created (in particular, the government) and therefore the size of claims is affected. An individual who possessed N units of currency C at the end of the year would possess the same after the end of the year. However, there now exist 1.05M units of C. Therefore, his claim has shrunk from N/M to N/1.05M, about a 5% drop.

This missing portion is now owned by the government. Hence, the size of people's claim on wealth is affected in reality—not just in measurement terms, as with a change of scale. Hence, an individual's wealth is decreased with C, and not with B. With C, he is less well off in real terms, and will not be able to undertake the same transactions he could with B. Hence, one can conclude that in C the size of claims represented by money is changed.

The situation with C is equivalent to the following two-stage process. First, make the same change as with B: a 5% increase in money, distributed in proportion to each person's moneyholdings. Second, enact a .05/1.05 tax on the money held by moneyholders. One sees that having the government (or indeed anyone) create money is equivalent to a tax on holding money. If a government does this, it is called "managing the money supply"—or sometimes "monetizing the deficit." If an individual does this, it is called counterfeiting and is subject to criminal prosecution. The motivations that cause a government to tax in such a devious manner will be examined later.

Since C is B combined with an annual .05/1.05 tax on moneyholding, real changes in the wealth of currency

C holders occur (not merely in the number which measures the price of a transaction), for a tax redistributes wealth. (The hypothesis that a tax also reduces the creation of wealth by reducing incentives to produce is also true, unproven here and not necessary to the present argument.)

With currency D, uncertainty exists as to the future scale of measurement provided by money. This uncertainty can be partially overcome in two ways. One could hold less money and more real assets, and engage in fewer monetary transactions. This minimizes both one's exposure to uncertainty and one's loss to the creation of a money tax. This strategy is suitable for one individual, but not everyone simultaneously— someone must hold the money. The cost, albeit an invisible one, is a loss of the extra creation of wealth achieved by the efficiency of monetary transactions. Second, because the average long-term annual increase in money is 14.6%,[1] one could form futures markets effectively selling insurance as to the future scale of measurement of money. Operation of the futures markets requires the consumption of real resources— the cost of this option.

Hence, uncertain increases in currency impose real costs on an economy, if only in the invisible form of opportunity costs.

Future markets will function efficiently if one can predict the long-run average annual increase in currency. With D, this is possible due to the idealized nature of the experiment. In real life, it is not. As the uncertainty increases, the cost of buying insurance becomes prohibitive, and eventually this option is eliminated. Thus, in situations with highly uncertain

---

[1] $\sqrt{1.05 \times 1.25} - 1$

increascs in currency, individuals have no option but to search for some alternative form of money, or let money fall into desuetude and revert to barter.

A portrays the ideal monetary system. B adds a pointless complication; however, there is little real cost. C demonstrates the true nature of currency increase—all to the government (in 1986, this tax raised $15 billion). D demonstrates the cost of uncertain increases. It is a sad commentary that the real world situation is even more uncertain than that of D.

In comparing the prices of similar transactions—that is, transactions involving the same goods—occurring at different times, in the same monetary system, one must deal with two effects. First is the strictly monetary effect of a change in scale of money. Second is changes in people's preferences, production methods, wealth, knowledge, etc. (changes that occur in the real world over time regardless of the change or lack of change in the monetary scale). Merely observing two specific prices at different times gives no way to determine the effect of each of these factors. For example, knowing that one paid $30 per barrel of oil in 1985 and $3 in 1972 does not allow one to conclude anything about changes in the scale of money, nor anything concerning the real prices paid for oil. The increase could be due to inflation, changes in the oil market, or a combination of the two.

If one knows only that the unit of measurement of distance (the foot) is changing over time, then a successive series of measurements of the size of a changing object conveys no information. One needs to know the nature of the change in scale before one can conclude even if the object is growing or shrinking.

Rational monetary policy requires no increase or decrease in the quantity of currency. Such increase or decrease accomplishes nothing, confuses things unnecessarily, and cannot be achieved in the real world without tangible costs. It provides no benefits. The sole reason increases are intentionally made each year, as shown with currency C, is to provide a means for the government to exact a tax in a highly invisible manner.

A constant money unit increases the range and scale of economic activity that can be undertaken. Without a constant money unit there exists a limit in time to the range of economic calculation, beyond which one risks choosing less efficient production alternatives. Thus inflation incurs the opportunity cost of a long-range loss of wealth creation, a cost borne by everyone and one with no countervailing benefit.

The foregoing is the definition of inflation, not a theory, or a method of computing it, or an opinion. This definition defines precisely the effect of changes of scale in money. Inflation is strictly a monetary phenomenon. It tells one nothing about unemployment, gross national product, price level, or any one of the other numbers economists like to play with.

If inflation is a constant 10% per year (currency increases 10% each year) then the price of a given transaction at time-t years is 1.1^t times higher than it would have been had that same transaction occurred with inflation equal to 0. The reason is solely a change in scale. It does not mean that the real price (% of total currency used in this transaction) is higher or lower. It does not say anything about any transactions, involving the same or different goods, which occurred at a different time. Specifically it does *not* say that the price of this transaction is 1.1^t times the price of a similar transaction at time 0.

Inflation is totally within the control of man. It is independent of any particular trader and is not affected by the prices of any particular transaction. There is absolutely no reason for inflation to be anything but zero. One is tempted to think that, if monetarist economists were in charge of architecture, they would decree that all yardsticks must grow 2% in length each year in order to keep up with the expanding size of buildings. The confusion is between a scale of measurement and a specific measurement of a given entity—a transaction.

In complicated production systems, economic calculations must be made across time; any given capital investment may take years to achieve a return. With a constant money system, one is assured that one's estimated measurements of future activity have an objectively verifiable meaning. Without constant money there exists a much smaller limit to the scale of economic activity one can undertake, beyond which one risks choosing less efficient economic alternatives with consequent loss of potential wealth.

Inflation cannot be measured by comparing the prices of different sets of transactions at different times in a given monetary system. Yet the entire present-day "science" of inflation (CPI, PPI, GNP Deflator) concentrates on this false issue. Inflation by itself gives no information whatsoever about the prices of different transactions at different times (or "prices" of goods).

Ordinary people have a great deal more experience with a given monetary system over time than they have dealing with different monetary systems. People remember what they used to pay for things, but have no direct experience with what things would now cost had the monetary system been handled differently. Hence, a great deal of nonsense concerning inflation has remained unchallenged.

Modern economists make two major errors concerning inflation. One, they compute it based on prices of specific transactions. This leads directly to price control as a means of preventing inflation—a feckless policy if the government insists on creating currency. Two, economists include credit as money (monetarists) and base their inflation policy on controlling (via legal means) credit use. Of course, some economists manage to make both errors simultaneously. These errors are examined in detail later.

Chapter Six

The Management of Money and Credit

Many institutions exist for the purpose of managing money and credit because modern economic life requires numerous ongoing decisions regarding these entities. One must distinguish between the management of money, the management of the monetary system, and the management of credit. After studying the institutions which currently perform these tasks, one discovers several startling inadequacies. One can then draw conclusions concerning the manner in which these entities ought to be managed.

Private banks evolved from providers of security for

cash to traders of credit. Money plays a very small role in a modern bank. The annual reports of large money-center banks reveal that cash represents less than 10% of total bank assets. This cash is used for transactional and reserve purposes only. Today banks are market-makers in credit; they trade credit on their own account. Banks also broker credit: arrange introduction of creditor and debtor for a fee. In addition, banks offer a sophisticated array of financial services. Banks do provide security in the form of safe-deposit boxes, a remnant of their original business. However, money has little to do with the actual operation of a modern bank.

That banks exist, on the scale they do, implies they serve an economic function. Credit is an economic entity, as legitimate as guns or butter. People who trade in credit provide real economic benefits for their customers—or else their customers would not support their activities. These benefits derive from economies of scale in banks' operations and from the sophisticated management of credit risk. Taxation and regulation have obscured these functions to the point where most individuals and many economists do not understand the role of banks.

A specific example of this ignorance can be found in the modern claim that banks "create money."

Most economists speak of the "multiplier effect" in which an initial increase in deposits at one bank is lent and re-lent throughout the banking system creating additional deposits many times (multiplying) the size of the initial deposit. This multiplier effect is the mechanism by which banks "create money." By examining the very example purporting to illustrate this creation of money, one sees the falsity of these claims. Private banks (banks owned by individuals as opposed to the State) do not create money.

Consider an individual, X, who deposits $1000 in Bank A. Specifically, he opens a checking account, also known as a demand deposit—for he can demand any or all of his money back at any time. He buys a promise to pay from the bank, a promise payable on the depositor's demand. These promissory notes usually sell at no discount (pay no interest), although recent high inflation is changing this practice. The bank often confers other privileges: the ability to write checks to a third party to be drawn on the depositor's account, preferential loan rates, or free investment advice. Note the following distinction: if the bank merely put the physical currency in a vault (as in a safe-deposit box), it would be providing protection only. The depositor would still own the money he deposits, although the bank would physically possess it. That depositor bears no credit risk. However, in X's case, the depositor no longer owns the money he deposits—the bank does. The depositor owns a promissory note issued by the bank, a piece of paper entitling him to certain rights. He has assumed credit risk; he is counting on the bank's ability to repay. The bank, which now owns the money, uses it as it wills: buying real estate, bonds, government securities, etc. A prudent bank will leave some currency idle, in reserve, to honor depositors' demands for cash. Economic realities, not government regulation, cause it to do this. Government regulation can affect only the level of these reserves.

In summary, when X deposits $1000 in cash into Bank A, he holds a promissory note with a face value of $1000. The bank has the cash—but not for long. The bank's accounts are as follows:

Bank A

Assets		Liabilities	
Asset	*Value*	*Liabilty*	*Value*
$1000 Cash	$1000	Promissory Note (due X)	$1000
	$1000		$1000

Bank A does not need to maintain $1000 in reserve against $1000 in deposits—typically a reserve of 10% will do. Recall that a bank accepts deposits from many depositors, all acting unilaterally. It is exceedingly unlikely that all would choose to withdraw their cash at one time.

Bank A has an incentive to relend a portion of the $1000 to people in need of financial credit—the interest it can charge on these loans. Suppose it lends $900 in cash to a second individual, Y, and charges interest; it buys a promise to pay. The bank's accounts now look like this.

Bank A

Assets		Liabilities	
Asset	*Value*	*Liabilty*	*Value*
$100 Cash	$100	Promissory Note (due X)	$1000
Promissory Note (from Y)	$900		
	$1000		$1000

The $1000 listed on the liability side is not money. It is the face value of the promissory note the bank sold. Do not confuse anything accountants write with money. Any bank's annual report contains terms like "provisions for bad debt" and "extraordinary loan loss." Accountants use these technical terms when they discover certain promissory notes are worth less than face value. Even the accountant must eventually concede money and promises to pay are separate entities. In general, the numbers listed under "value" on both sides of the accounts do not represent money—they are the monetary value or price paid for the entity listed under "asset" or "liability." The value of $100 cash is $100. The price paid for the note due from Y is $900.

The mini-economy of X, Y, and Bank A still has $1000 cash in it. Bank A owns $100 cash, Y has $900 cash and X has none. In addition, there are two promissory notes; credit has been created. Banks and individuals can create credit at will—anyone using a credit card to purchase something creates credit. Banks' raison d'etre is to create economic activity by facilitating trade in promises to pay. However, no money has been created.

Continuing with the example, one might suppose Y deposits his $900 in Bank B (or, equivalently, Y buys something from Z and Z deposits the $900 in Bank B). Bank B keeps $90 cash in reserve, and lends $810 to W, leaving its statement as follows:

Bank B

Assets		Liabilities	
Asset	*Value*	*Liabilty*	*Value*
$90 Cash	$ 90	Promissory Note	$900
Promissory Note (from W)	$810	(due Y)	
	$900		$900

We can assume that this process of redepositing and relending continues indefinitely with new depositors, borrowers, and banks. If the reserve ratio used is 10% then 10% of the cash stays in each bank.

Because politicians, economists, and bankers do not understand the distinction between credit and money, they conclude the banking system has created money. They do this by adding the face values (prices paid) of the banks' outstanding promises to pay, instead of the amounts of cash present. This addition, it can be shown by elementary arithmetic, will total $10,000.[1] Economists then speak of the multiplier effect which turned $1000 into $10,000. This is wishful thinking and equivocation. If one looks for money, one will find $100 cash in Bank A, $90 cash in Bank B, $81 cash in Bank C, etc., and that those amounts of money total $1000 cash—the same amount of money individual X started with, now in the hands of new owners.

Banks create wealth. They serve an economic function by doing things (managing credit risk) more efficiently than would otherwise be possible.

Banks create credit. They do this by buying or selling promises to pay.

Banks do not create money. The only entity with that power is the government. Anyone else trying is guilty of counterfeiting.

The creation of credit by banks is a productive enterprise in which all participating parties hope to benefit, and in which non-participating parties are not directly affected. The creation of money by the government represents a forcible, non-voluntary, and unilateral transfer of wealth from those who hold a general, objectively verifiable claim on wealth (moneyholders)

---

[1] $1,000/10%

to those who run the printing press (the government). In short, a tax.

A bank that could truly create money would be exacting a tax on all moneyholders. No such private institutions exist. No economist would claim that banks create gold—yet gold can be a form of money.

The false claim that private banks create money was the intellectual source of government regulation of banks. These regulations are wide ranging. Regulation Q imposes legal limits on the interest rates banks can pay their depositors. The reserve requirements force banks to maintain artificially high levels of reserves. Direct interstate retail banking is prohibited. Banks' legal positions vary with size—"large" banks pay a different rate for federal funds than "small" banks. Political jawboning (direct threats of punitive legislation) forces banks into courses of action they would not otherwise take.

Undoubtedly, there exist instances in which banks engage in fraudulent, misleading and corrupt practices in which the property rights of individuals are abrogated. These cases should be tried under an objective judicial system with severe criminal penalties for convicted parties. To use such cases as political rationale to force regulation on all banks is to convict all gun-owners of murder. Undoubtedly, there also exist instances in which poorly run banks are unable to honor their depositors' requests for funds and so go bankrupt. This is part of the risk of extending credit to a bank. It is no basis for legal, forcible regulation, control, and insurance of private banks by the state. Depositors who wish to avoid these risks should use a safe-deposit box.

A central bank is a government agency originally created to monitor and manage the nation's money supply—namely, the gold in circulation and later paper, issued for transactional convenience, supposedly convertible into gold. In the United States, the central bank is called the Federal Reserve (Fed).

After the central banks' creation, two events occurred. The government accumulated gold for its own account, used initially to insure the convertibility of paper currency into gold. Also, the paper which the central bank issued as legal tender (paper money—a proxy for gold, or a claim to specific gold) became confused with the paper (notes of credit) issued by private banks.

These developments had two consequences. First, the government realized that, by printing paper, it could exact an invisible tax, something not possible with gold currency. Eventually this issuance of multiple claims on the same gold forced the government to cease honoring the convertibility of paper to gold (the U.S. Government went so far as the outlaw the ownership of gold for a period of time). Second, the confusion of paper money with paper credit allowed the government to assume regulatory control (via the central bank) of private banks under the guise of "managing the money supply." Government power expanded enormously.

The true function of the Fed has nothing to do with the money supply. Its purpose is to regulate the affairs of private banks. Less tactfully but more honestly, the Fed is in the business of abrogating the property rights of individuals—specifically of those individuals who own banks and indirectly of those individuals who do business with banks.

Economists claim the function of the Fed is to control the money supply or to control interest rates. This is apocryphal. Ultimately, the entity that manages the money supply and influences a great portion of the credit markets is Congress. Congress has the constitutional power to determine laws that decide government revenues (taxes, T) and government expenditures (G). Normally, as in the last twenty years save one, T is less than G and the government is in deficit. There exist three ways to cover this deficit: the sale of assets (rarely used), government borrowing (currently greater than two trillion dollars), and the creation of currency. Congress directly controls all these factors except the last. The Fed causes the creation of currency at the implicit request of the Treasury but has no say over the amount. If it issued less currency than required by Congress, checks issued by the Treasury would bounce, an alternative not "politically feasible."

Congress has three direct conflicts of interest in its role as the nation's money manager. When Congress causes the creation of additional currency, it:

a. exacts an inflationary tax on moneyholders since the government owns the newly minted currency;

b. increases the average income-tax rate due to bracket creep, a consequence of progressive income tax rates;

c. cheats government creditors (e.g., pension funds and banks) by devaluing the dollars with which it pays back government debt.

Only the naive expect Congress to do a responsible job under these circumstances.

One loser is the Fed itself. It is saddled with the political responsibility for the effects of money management, a process it does not control. Today the Fed is engaged in ridiculous and nugatory attempts either to "cool an overheated economy" by legally (forcibly) cutting back on the so-called money-supply growth (the growth of credit) or to "stimulate a recessionary economy" by injecting reserves into the banking system (easing credit regulations or printing money). Credit, the lifeblood of a productive economy, is being stifled so that Congress can continue to print a flood of depreciating paper money to pay for its follies. Congress extirpates the nation's currency and creates inflation at the same time it limits private credit, so that its own false measures of "money" remain in line.

Credit does not cause inflation.

High interest rates do not cause inflation.

One does not control inflation by controlling any specific prices, whether those paid for credit or for any other commodity.

The government has no moral business regulating any aspect of credit: its quantity, its price, or its form. To do so serves no productive end. The only effect of such action, apart from the camouflaging of government property theft by money creation, is to further destroy freedom in economic life, with disastrous long-term consequences.

What is the proper role of the Fed?

Suppose the Fed ceased to create currency (other than to replace physically deteriorated currency returned by banks, to issue only replacement currency) and ceased to regulate private credit. The following desirable consequences would occur.

Inflation would immediately cease. It would be zero by definition.

The inflationary tax on moneyholders would cease.

The productive use of credit would flower, provided

the government did not try to insulate creditors from the risks of granting credit as it now does via depositors' insurance.

The economy would grow rapidly but would not "overheat."

Congress would be forced to contend with and accept political responsibility for its own deficit, being unable to monetize it.

Of course this will not happen, the Fed being subject to Congress's control.

The foregoing is not meant to suggest that the Fed should in fact be responsible for the nation's monetary system, only that it could do a far better job. An outline of, and the means of operation for, the ideal monetary system follow.

The key to a perfect form of money is an absolutely fixed total amount of currency. There being no commodity in nature with this property, man must create one. Money represents a claim on economic goods and services that is measureable and objective (not being subject to the action or inaction of any specific person). The essential feature is the information, the size of the claim on goods and services, that the ownership of a currency unit represents. To create an ideal form of money, one must somehow create a fixed number of these claims.

The solution depends on considering the claims before dwelling on the physical currency. One arbitrarily fixes a total amount of UTC (say 100 billion). One can do this arbitrarily because of the device of proportionality. The appropriate number is determined so as to insure that ordinary transactions in everyday life are measured in human-sized numbers, one to one hundred. In order to permanently fix the number of these units, one numbers them consecutively from one to one hundred billion, assigning a unique serial number to each.

To indicate the size of a transaction, one needs to know how many units are being transferred. To track ownership, make the trade, and simultaneously insure a permanently fixed number of units, one needs to know which specific units one is referring to. The rule that one unit can and must be owned by one and only one person at any given time is sufficient to make this system work.

To this point all is abstract. One must yet make the monetary system concrete (coin the currency). Billions of transactions are made everyday and billions of currency units are exchanged everyday, so one needs a complex system to handle the recording of ownership. While not possible today, the near future should see the development of information systems with sufficient capacity to record all the nation's transactions.[2]

To make a monetary transaction, two steps are involved. First, ownership of the good or service being bought or sold is transferred. Second, the information system transfers ownership of the appropriate number of monetary units from the person buying to the person selling.

How would this system work in practice? A large interconnected network of computers would work on a single central file. This file would consist of a record for every currency unit containing the serial number of

---

[2]   In developing such a system, a plausible approach would be to segment the market of all transactions according to transaction size and target the big ones first. As the system develops in sophistication, progressively smaller transactions could be included. For transactions not yet included, a less-perfect form of money such as precious or semi-precious metal coins could be used.

that unit and the name or number of the current owner. Millions of terminals scattered around the country would feed in transactions, changes in ownership of specific units. Terminals would need the capacity to recognize specific individuals or corporations; whether by identity card, signature recognition, or fingerprint is irrelevant. A transaction would be effected by the simultaneous entry by two individuals of the amount and the identity of the trading partners. After verifying that the buyer had sufficient cash in his name, the change in ownership would occur and a hardcopy record would be produced. Elaborate backup systems would be required to provide the requisite security and system integrity. (Those who wonder where the physical commodity referred to in the definition of money can be found in the system should note that the magnetic fields in whatever storage device the computers use represent the actual currency).

What difficulties and objections exist in implementing this sytem? The following prolepsis will dispose of the major ones.

First, one could object to the enormous cost of the required information system, hardware and software. Both the capital and operating costs of this system are decreasing rapidly with every advance in electronics technology. The hardware cost per transaction has been decreasing exponentially over the past three decades and shows every indication of continuing this trend. However, regardless of future cost trends, the system would pay for itself or fail. It is not being proposed that the government set up, control, or manage this system, financing the effort with tax dollars, thereby freeing the system from economic realities. It is being proposed that the system be privately run and funded by private investors who expect a return. System users would be willing to pay for its use, either directly or indirectly through patronizing businesses that use the system, because of the enormous economic advantages this monetary system provides.

Second, one could object to the size of the required system by claiming it is not technologically possible to build such a system even if we could afford it. The fact that technology is not available today does not preclude its existence tomorrow. Rapid advances occur continuously. It is not necessary to construct the whole system at once. One could ease into it as the technology became available—for example, by the method indicated in Footnote Two on page 80. The system is not required to handle all economic transactions, only those involving cash. The majority of all transactions are credit transactions. Practically all business-to-business transactions are credit transactions; even the so-called "cash on delivery" usually involves a check or at most a certified check. The majority of consumer-related transactions involve credit. Witness the proliferation of credit devices: checks, credit cards, debit cards, travelers' checks, EFT, charge cards, direct payroll deposits, etc. Typically, people use cash for small transactions, for illegal transactions for which anonymity is required, and for some transactions with banks. The widespread use of credit is an enormous simplification. As the sophistication of information systems grows, the use of credit should spread, further decreasing the use of cash. However, cash must always exist, else there is no way to value (price) credit transactions.

Third, one could object to the enormous centralization of information, the lack of privacy, and the potential security abuses inherent in this system. However, no one is forced to use the system. One is free to not trade, to barter or to use credit exclusively. It is not seriously suggested that one would confine oneself to these methods, only that those options exist. There are tremendous economic advantages to using money. One cannot expect to reap enormous economic benefits without cost. The problem singled out by this objection is that an objective record would exist of all monetary transactions one entered and that the amount of cash one owned would be highly visible. If one judges this cost too great, one can choose not to own money. Private ownership and management of this system would prevent most of the abuses. Its investors are concerned with marketing a product whose value stems from its certainty, objectivity, and continuity. They would do everything possible to uphold these values. In contrast, consider the alternative: a State-run system. The State has no direct economic incentive to uphold the system's integrity, every economic and political incentive to abuse the system, and a monopoly on the legal use of force to achieve its wishes. This last reason alone is sufficient for prohibiting State involvement in the monetary system. This basic objection could just as easily be applied to the use of credit cards. The existence of hundreds of millions of credit cards testifies to the lack of merit most Americans see in this objection.

Fourth, one could point to the possibility of theft by the owners. They could easily create a few extra units, in effect counterfeiting money for their own use. The objectivity and visibility of the system prevent this from happening. One cannot create a unit with a serial number outside the given range; no one would accept it. One cannot create a duplicate serial number; sooner or later, both identical units would show up in one transaction. Before one claims that the chance of this is small, especially if only a "few" extra units were created, let us examine the cost of such an action. If a single such event occurred and were made public knowledge, it would instantly and completely destroy all faith in the monetary system, thereby entirely annihilating the system owners' investment. This enormous economic incentive is what upholds the system's integrity. Note that no such incentive exists with today's State-controlled money system, and that the government does not shirk from each year creating billions of extra dollars for its own account. If a private money system tried one-ten-thousandth of the counterfeiting the government routinely indulges in, the outcry would be deafening and the owners' investment would cease to exist. All the government's laws cannot begin to approach this sort of protection for the individual.

These objections aside, what of the advantages of such a system? How does its operation provide the return necessary to pay for its operating costs?

The advantages arise because this physical system implements exactly all the essential elements indicated in the definition of money. It represents exactly the ideal form of money. The cardinal element of this idealness is the absolutely fixed number of currency units. Byproducts of this fixity are the impossibility of counterfeit currency, an inflation rate of zero by definition, the lack of any wealth transfer to the government via the inflation tax, and the lack of any risk or uncertainty in holding currency.

This money system is designed to provide objectivity, stability over time, and security, qualities totally absent from current monetary systems. A great deal of man's effort is directed towards the attainment of these ends in various contexts. The opportunity to use a currency with absolute security and lasting value is something most men would pay well for. The developers of such a system have the responsibility of converting this desire into investment reality—strictly a business problem. The market is there, it only need be exploited.

The use of this monetary system does not preclude the use of credit; if anything, it encourages credit. It does, however, illustrate further the distinction between money and credit.

While a unit standard of measurement is fundamental to money's objectivity, no such unit exists for credit. Moreover, credit can be objectively measured only in economies where money exists (via the price mechanism, the price of a promise to pay).

A creditor always bears the risk of nonrepayment: the value of his promissory note is dependent upon the actions of the promisor. Its value is subjective and not necessarily transferable, let alone transferable at face value. In contrast, the moneyholder bears no risk derived from the action or inaction of any specific individual. By the very nature of money, its value to a moneyholder is objective and transferable.

Both the creditor and moneyholder bear the uncertainty of not knowing in advance what their claim (in the case of the creditor, his claim if and when redeemed) will buy. That depends on the productivity and knowledge of their fellow men, the wealth of society.

Chapter Seven

Multicurrency Systems

International trade occurs daily in great measure. Aside from political difficulties and ramifications, international trade raises an interesting economic question. How is it possible to conduct monetary transactions (or monetary credit transactions) if the two traders involved deal with different monetary systems? Since money provides a scale of measurement, how can one reconcile the two scales of measurement provided by two different currencies? If nations are to progress beyond autarchy, these questions are important.

Consider an American who wishes to import Japanese cars. Suppose the Japanese manufacturer has hitherto engaged in an entirely domestic operation, not having exported its product. Immediately a problem of currency arises. The Japanese does not want to accept dollars for his cars; they are valueless pieces of paper in Japan and no one will accept them as payment for goods or services. Dollars are not legal tender in Japan. The American cannot pay the Japanese with yen, for he receives dollars for the cars he sells. Unless some common ground can be found, international trade seems to have reached an impasse. To say that the international banks will handle the currency exchange is a non-answer. This approach merely assigns the problem to new owners. One may as well confront the issue directly.

A historical solution to this problem (dating from antiquity to August 15, 1971) was the use of gold as an international currency. Being largely outside the control of governments, gold was thought to be suitably objective and stable for international trade. Not that gold was used directly by the car importer in America or the car producer in Japan—banks and central banks generally handled these details. Gold provided an objective way to value claims and hence was acceptable to both trading partners. Gold in America was substantially the same as gold in Japan, whereas dollars and yen differed in amount, value, controlling entity, and legal status. Hence, the scale of measurement afforded was identical in America and in Japan. Without gold (or a similar entity), international trade would be reduced to barter.

In the wider context of generalized international trade (trade involving two economies with different currencies), the fundamental problem is to determine the exchange rate—a factor that connects the two different scales of measurement—which will allow economic value to be made objective to both trading partners.

From this specific example, two general conclusions can be drawn. First, exchange rates can exist only if direct or indirect international monetary trade exists. If no goods were imported or exported from Japan there would be no exchange rate to convert yen into any other currency. An exact analogy is any priceless object—one that has had no price (not infinite price— infinite price is a meaningless impossibility). Second, if international monetary trade exists, one must have a special currency, called a reserve currency. In the above example, the reserve currency is gold. The reserve currency provides the means with which to establish an exchange rate.

As mentioned, gold has been the historical reserve currency. Nations maintained large stocks of gold, used to conduct international trade. A nation that ran out of reserves was thought unable to import until it built its gold reserves back up by exporting goods, producing gold itself, or plundering it from some other, hapless nation. Powerful nations, such as England or Spain in the sixteenth, seventeenth, and eighteenth centuries, sought out new sources of gold in the New World. Rapid influxes of new gold, if introduced into circulation by government spending (as was usually the case), caused rampant inflation. Spain experienced this after conquering the Aztecs and the Incas. Mistaken ideas as to the true value of gold (as money) led to inflation, false ideas as to the nature of wealth, and poor management of international trade.

Eventually, paper money was introduced domestically for transactional convenience. This paper was directly convertible to gold—therefore as "good as gold." Paper money eventually worked its way into international trade, but only if backed by a general trust in the issuing government. In the nineteenth and early twentieth centuries the international currency was the British pound. Later the American dollar took over. Exchange rates, at first directly pegged (regulated by law) and later priced by market forces, existed converting other currencies to the American dollar. The required objectivity existed because the American dollar was directly convertible to gold at a set rate, 1/35 of an ounce per one dollar, thereby indirectly setting up rates for the conversion of other currencies to gold. In practice, these dollars were rarely traded in for gold; people liked the convenience of paper. Because they trusted the American Government, and its large stocks of gold in Fort Knox, they were satisfied to hold paper.

This trust was ill-placed. The conflict of interest between economic policy and political reality caused Congress to produce a sea of paper which, if converted to gold, would have severely damaged the American economy.

The gold system died on August 15, 1971 under the direction of President Nixon. He had no choice—the official price of gold (the rate at which dollars would be redeemed in gold) was $35 per ounce, but the free market prices being paid for gold were around $100 per ounce. One could make a tidy profit buying gold from the U.S. Government by redeeming dollars for gold at the official rate and then selling this gold on the international market for a much higher price. Each transaction would triple one's money, an eminently satisfactory rate of return. Needless to say, Americans were not allowed to own gold at this time. It is fascinating to ask: why did foreign governments not indulge in this profitable business?

The answer attests to the lunacy of political action

involving economics. Free-market prices paid for gold were increasing as Congress printed money to help cover its deficits. These dollars found their way into the hand of foreigners who used them as reserve currency. Foreign central banks were wary of low reserves, a legacy of the days when gold was used as the reserve currency. They liked to hold substantial reserves. In addition, a poor understanding of economics provided a powerful motivation for central banks to hold dollars rather than cash them in for gold. The dollars Congress printed caused inflation in America. The false conventional wisdom held that this discouraged German or Japanese exports to America, because the prices paid for these goods were high in nominal dollars. This conventional wisdom ignores the fact that American inflation affects all domestic prices by an equal factor. The Germans and Japanese, blind to the nature and causes of capital flows, decided that exports were "a good thing," again a false conclusion. Trade, whether import or export, is desirable in that it creates wealth; imports can be paid for via capital that flows into an expanding politically stable economy. The Germans and Japanese falsely assumed that American inflation impeded their exports. They therefore bought up the dollars Congress printed supposedly to reduce this inflation. By ending the dollar's convertibility to gold (closing the gold window), Nixon left the Germans and Japanese holding the bag, which contained mountains of paper. The German and Japanese strategy cost their citizens billions of dollars. It also cost Americans billions in subsequent lost foreign investment, an invisible but substantial cost.

Had the Germans and Japanese insisted on cashing in dollars for gold and not irrationally pursued exports and reserve accumulation, the Americans would have been left to pay for their own follies. More likely, the situation would never have reached the sad state it did.

Since August 1971, uncertainty has permeated the international monetary markets. The floating exchange rates (market determined), as well as the prices paid for gold, rise and fall with political rumor, election results, projected government deficits, and threats of war. No objective standard exists for international trade. Fixed exchange rates provide no solution. Only when people begin to understand the nature of cash will objectivity rule and international trade flourish.

Dollars spent on imports circulate outside the country. In a free country this is of no particular concern. These dollars do not represent a debt instrument such as Treasury Bonds. The external circulation of dollars does not mean Americans are beholden to foreigners in the sense they owe them anything. (Treasury Bonds, on the other hand, can represent a foreign liability of Americans.) Also, these dollars do not represent a large portion of American wealth now somehow "lost overseas." Taken together, all money is a small part of the wealth of America. It provides a scale to measure that wealth and its existence is instrumental in creating that wealth, but in and of itself the claim it represents is not a large part of American wealth.

There is no possibility, as xenophobic economists claim, that foreigners with export surpluses could end up controlling the majority of American dollars and then dictate the American economy. One cannot dictate a free economy. It is of no value for foreigners to accumulate American dollars and not reintroduce them to the economy via trade or capital flows. The only way in which a foreigner (or indeed anyone) could affect the American monetary system is to sell things and destroy the currency he receives. (Note that this is impos-

sible in the ideal monetary system outlined previously.)
To do so is equivalent to a wholesale transfer of wealth
to people who continue to hold dollars. If this is what
our trading "adversaries" wish to do, by all means let
them.

One can defuse the economic claims of trade protec-
tionists by examining the mechanics, at the individual
level, of international trade. For an individual to purchase foreign goods, there are but three ways to con-
summate an international transaction: an exchange of
real assets with the foreign partner, the borrowing of
money to buy, and the use of one's own cash. A trade of
assets is non-monetary; no currency or trade-deficit
issues arise. The trader would not trade unless he felt
the transaction would improve his situation. Any individual has a finite borrowing capacity; a lender will
lend only to the extent he feels he will be paid back.
Hence, an importer who finances his purchases with
borrowing can continue only to the extent he is creating wealth. A trader who pays cash for imports is
limited by the cash available. This cash would be used
up in approximately one year at today's trade-deficit
levels. However, long before this occurred, the relative
prices of import transactions to domestic transactions
would shift in favor of the domestic. By their nature,
trade imbalances are self-correcting.

If all trading nations simultaneously adopted gold
as currency, international money markets would disappear and prices could adjust in response to gold
flows. The balance of trade between nations would be
seen as no more important than say the balance of
trade between New York and California. Money is an
exceedingly liquid capital; it will flow to where it is best
treated: a free, capitalistic society. Clearly, the real
reason politicians and economists promulgate protec-

tionism to "cure" trade deficits or win trade "wars" is because free international trade would necessarily cause them to lose political control of money. Restrictions another country places on its imports or subsidies it grants to its exports have a deleterious effect on its citizens, not on Americans. If these restrictions are severe, capital flight will result. Real money will not tolerate political meddling.

The value of a dollar is in what it will buy, not in who owns it. A foreigner buying goods with American dollars is no different than any other monetary transaction. It results in a new owner of the same dollar. That is not the same as collecting an IOU.

These facts imply that balance of trade is economically insignificant. In a free society, any "imbalances" are self-correcting over time because of the special nature of money. The only rational foreign policy between nations practicing comity is free trade. It is both moral and economically sound. Government intervention in international trade (justified by these trade "imbalances") is disastrous. A government's universal reaction is to restrict trade via quotas, tariffs, duties, jawboning, etc. In other words, a government's reaction to a perceived loss of wealth is to destroy the most important mechanism for creating wealth—trade.

This analysis does not apply to the foreign ownership of government debt, which represents an obligation of all Americans. However, the significance of this debt is that it is debt, not that it is held by foreigners. It may be marginally preferable to owe money to Americans than to foreigners, but it is infinitely preferable for the government to owe no one.

International trade creates wealth for all parties involved; hence, it should not be impeded by state interventions in the form of tariffs, quotas, nationalizations, trigger prices, jawboning, or bilateral trade agreements. Capitalistic nations will enjoy more trade, and hence more wealth, than non-capitalistic ones.

Still, the problem of an objective international scale of measure exists. How can one compare the two scales of measurement provided by two different currencies?

The only way to compare two different scales of measurement is to measure the same thing with both scales and relate the results. If one knows that an object is two inches long and that the same object is also 50.8 millimeters long, then one knows that one inch equals 25.4 millimeters. Unfortunately, because of the nature of money and the nature of a transaction, this approach is not possible for currency. The exclusive use of one currency in a transaction precludes the use of another in that same transaction. Hence, no mathematically perfect comparison is possible.

The next best solution is to compare the measurements of similar things. One can compare different transactions involving similar goods occurring at about the same time. Preferably one should use commmodity-type goods with large, liquid, international markets: gold, steel, oil, or wheat. These commodities have a demonstrated record of being sold at near-uniform prices over short periods of time. One makes the assumption that prices paid in dollars for gold in New York should be approximately equal to prices paid in francs for gold in Zurich, if these prices occur on the same day. Arbitrage prevents large differences. Examining several such commodities would determine the approximate value of the exchange rate. Note that this is a market measurement rather than a theoretical calculation. International money markets are the concrete form of this measurement.

The proper answer to the original problem of the

American importer of Japanese cars is that any currency can serve as a "reserve currency," provided international money markets exist to trade in currency and determine exchange rates. These markets will exist if their participants (large, multinational, financial institutions) can make a profit by selling currency for a small premium over what they paid for it.

International traders will pay for this in order to derive the benefits of international trade. "Fixed" exchange rates are no more than State intervention in international money markets, the "multinationalization" of this industry. Its results are: legally determined as opposed to market-determined prices, loss of trading efficiency, loss of international trade, and loss of wealth. Perhaps the citizens of Germany and Japan would like to comment on the "benefits" of state intervention in the international money markets.

The only remaining question concerns the operation of international money markets: what factors affect the prices that the participants in these markets charge?

If two nations' economies are connected via international trade, two separate factors affect exchange rates. First is the amount of each currency and predicted additions to these amounts. All else being constant, a nation that undertook a planned, one-time, unilateral ten-percent increase in its currency base should see a ten-percent increase in the prices paid for foreign currency, a ten-percent increase over what the price would have been had there been no increase in the currency base. This is solely a logical consequence of the nature of money. Second, any factor affecting the wealth of a nation would affect the prices its citizens must pay to buy things. Hence, if some factor affected one nation but not another (for example, internal State intervention in its own economy), it should affect the exchange rate. That is why a state's fiscal policy, domestic trade regulation, and election results affect its exchange rate. Two wholly capitalistic nations, with stable currencies, should experience little exchange-rate fluctuations other than those due to acts of God or third-party aggression.

Because there today exist enormous legal and political barriers to international and domestic trade, one cannot compare standards of living in different countries by comparing average salaries and adjusting for exchange rates. One must know what a dollar will buy in America and what a yen will buy in Japan. The absence of totally free international trade allows the possibility that the difference in purchasing power may be other than the exchange rate would suggest.

Conventional analysis concerning the impact of trade deficits, current accounts, capital accounts, or interest rates on exchange rates is irrelevant. Some factors which affect rates may also affect these entities, but to claim these entities cause changes in exchange rates is simply false.

Part II
The Failure of
Modern Economics

Chapter Eight

Failures of Analysis

People refer to economics as the dismal science; even this derogatory description is too generous by half. While dismal, economics is far from science. Modern economics is devoid of valid, consistent definitions, uses no objective scales of measurement, does not conduct scientific experiment, and is not able to make predictions. Any valid science must embody all these characteristics. Modern economics consists of imprecise terms, inaccurate descriptive observations, and untestable, invalid, ad hoc theories with no basis in reality. Calculation has replaced thought; mysticism and whim have replaced valid conceptual integration of observed facts. Specific examples of these charges follow.

Why have economists let this state of affairs exist? How has economics become the alchemy of the twentieth century?

Economics suffers the effects of invalid epistemology. Its method of acquiring knowledge is not valid; therefore, its conceptual content is meaningless.

99

Economic theory and economic practice are forever severed. Economic theory deliberately does not pertain to facts of reality. The descriptive facts economists observe are never integrated into valid concepts. Economics suffers from an old (and false) philosophic dichotomy: rationalism versus empiricism. Its source is the notion that man's mind is not competent to deal with reality. The logical outcome of such a policy is the unreality of current economic thought.[1]

This thesis is best illustrated by the three examples which make up this chapter. In each, one sees that the concepts which form the so-called theory are not grounded in reality (their definitions are not valid). Hence, the conclusions these theories reach are meaningless.

The "Law" of Supply and Demand
(The Non-Science of Microeconomics)

In every introductory economics text, one will see the following diagram:

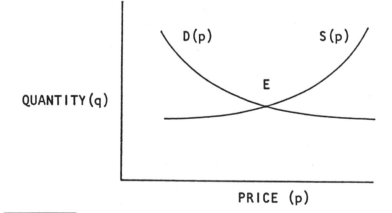

---

[1] This observation comes from M. Buechner, writing in *The Objectivist Forum* (August 1982).

The demand function gives the quantity D(p) of a specific good that would be demanded at any particular price p. The supply function gives the quantity S(p) of that same good that would be supplied at any particular price p. The global context is not clear. Presumably this graph refers to a specified set of traders trading for a specific period of time. At any rate, the intersection point of these two graphs is called the equilibrium point, and is supposed to give the price and quantity of trade that will occur in the unstated global context. Economists calculate the elasticity of demand (or supply) by dividing the percent change in quantity by the percent change in price. A good whose demand changes rapidly with price is said to be elastic; one whose demand changes slowly is said to be inelastic.

If, as in this case, the supply and demand curves are calculated for a single commodity, this model is offered as a method of determining the price of a particular commodity. In order to make the model dynamic, economists start moving the supply or demand curves around, thereby changing the equilibrium price. The notion of equilibrium begs the concept disequilibrium, and with it a whole set of theory and policies concerning how one gets from disequilibrium to equilibrium. One assumes that equilibrium is "good" and that disequilibrium is "bad."

Economists generalize this model so as to apply it to all goods and services (aggregate demand and supply). With it they attempt to predict the income level, employment level, and price level of entire economies without so much as a word as to the appropriate scale of measurement for any of these quantities. In its equilibrium form, this aggregate model is the basis of classical economics. With the wild card of disequilibrium, it becomes the theoretical basis for Keynesianism.

Keynesianism assumes one has to globally "manage" aggregate supply and demand to make them "come out equal," so as to be at equilibrium (full employment).

The "law" of supply and demand is the common thread through all economics since Adam Smith's. It is also the common reason why such economics are invalid.

There is no law of supply and demand. It suffers from the use of undefined terms and the existence of self-contradictions. This "law" ignores the role of money and the actual nature of a transaction. It is not science but numerology.

What are the specific shortcomings and objections?

First, the so-called supply and demand functions are imaginary. They do not exist and are not measurable. Every point on a demand or supply curve represents prices that do not exist for transactions that never occurred. Economists cannot guarantee that the two curves will even intersect. Economists claim that a demand function gives the amount of a good that would be demanded at a given price. One can measure only what is, not what would be. Subjunctive measurements have no place in science. Do economists propose we measure demand curves via public-opinion polls? How do they guarantee people will do as they say they will? If not via public-opinion polls, then how? If one asserts that a supply curve is only a theoretical construct (cannot be applied to reality), what use is it? Try to pin down an economist as to the demand for wheat at \$1.72/bushel or the elasticity of Oldsmobile Cutlasses at \$12,000/car. As soon as one tries to get specific, one realizes the supply and demand curves say nothing.

Second, a price is a measurement of the size of a monetary transaction, not the attribute of a good. This may seem a trifling objection; however, it is a profound one. No good or service is homogeneous. Wheat comes in different varieties and protein contents; cars come in numerous sizes, shapes, and models. Even so fungible a commodity as gold commands different prices depending on where you buy it: Zurich, London, or New York. Its asked or bid price is also a function of when you buy or sell it. A price is a measurement of the size of a monetary transaction; a transaction is the exchange of ownership of two specified pieces of property between two specified people at a specified time. If any element is missing, no price is defined. No good, per se, has a price. The attribution of price and therefore value to goods is in direct contradiction to the fact that value can arise only in the context of man. The attribution of price to transactions encounters no such difficulty. It makes no sense to speak of the demand for a good at a price. One must know by whom and when. This confusion (even economists have noted the diversity of prices of transactions involving similar goods) has led to the false notions of a natural, fair, or equilibrium price, a futile attempt to integrate these different observed prices into the "price of a good." For, in postulating the existence of the price of a good, economists recognize that they must explain its determining factors. The "law of supply and demand" is a false attempt to explain the determination of a non-existent entity.

Third, no global context is defined for the analysis; specifically, time is ignored. Does the supply-demand analysis represent the situation at an instantaneous point in time? Must one conclude that two transactions occurring at the same time, involving the same goods, must have the same price? Does the supply-demand analysis cover a specific period of time, with a definite

beginning and end? Must one conclude that the supply
and demand curves are immutable for that period, that
people cannot change their minds over that time? Must
all transactions occur at the same price per unit of
good? Is the supply of a good the amount that exists,
the amount that could be produced or the amount that
could be produced after more investment in capital
goods? Or perhaps the supply-demand analysis is
meant to occur over time, but not a specified period?
What happens after the equilibrium quantity of the
good is bought and sold? The curves become identically
equal to zero? Trade ceases?

Fourth, the analysis assumes that the supply and
demand functions are the causal mechanism which
determines prices. Even if we ignore the fact that prices
are ascribed to the wrong entity, this still is not true.
The price of a transaction is determined solely by the
two people engaging in it, by comparing the proposed
transaction to the available alternatives. The motor is
man's mind. Other similar transactions occurring
elsewhere may influence the traders by providing a
benchmark (what others think), but these transactions
do not determine the price. One always has a choice,
even if only not to buy (sell).

Fifth, no appropriate scales of measurement are
used. On the price axis, changes in the quantity of
currency over time are ignored, so no unit is defined.
On the quantity axis, it is assumed that all commodities are quantifiable on a single scale: physical amount
(number of units or weight). How can services be measured? Shall one measure the consultant's reports by the
number of pages? Shall one measure an architect's
services by the number of bricks he sketches? Or is the
supply-demand analysis not suited to the pricing of
transactions involving services? Would one then con-

clude that all electronic calculators are equal, to be priced equally? Again this objection is not trivial. One must either be willing to group entities that are not identical to get a commodity, or insist that each individual existent is a commodity.

Last, this model attempts to explain the price and quantity of trade in isolation, as if no other goods or services need be considered, a fundamentally false approach. People are able to reach agreement on price precisely because alternative courses of action are available. In their complete absence price would be meaningless since price is predicated upon choice. There have been attempts to modify supply and demand curves by factors that take account of, for example, the purchasing power lost if one buys the commodity in question or the range of competing goods available. Each and all of these approaches mistakenly attempts to measure traders' decisions before they occur in order to quantitatively relate different demand curves. The entire analysis of supply and demand is a futile attempt to measure transactions that did not occur. The underlying reality of trade is the transactions that did occur, and they can be measured (if monetary) by price.

Observe the devastating and pervasive consequences of the false identification of the law of supply and demand.

Economists deduce the existence of a fair, natural, or equilibrium price (presumably for each good or service; this is a result of the invalid attempt to integrate the prices of several similar transactions). Economists arbitrarily assert the existence of this norm, and are unable to propose any method of discerning the norm from the abnormal. This error causes much injustice and hardship, for its obvious conclusion is that prices

that are not natural, fair, or in equilibrium are not right
and therefore immoral, and so should be made illegal.
In one fell swoop, economists provide the intellectual
justification for the non-concepts of surplus wealth,
price fixing, price gouging, predatory pricing, price
control, and antitrust laws. By applying the false
supply-demand analysis to markets instead of goods,
economists produce invalid notions such as natural
monopoly, oligopoly, and cartel, with the implicit
assumption that in these situations "competition" is
somehow "not perfect" and should be regulated. When
applied to a whole economy, the false normative concept of equilibrium becomes the basis and justification
for attempts to "manage the economy." There is no
moral or economic basis for any of these conclusions.
The identification of any economic norms is false and
invalid.

When norms replace objective measures, one is not
allowed to question the nature of things. Education is a
good thing; therefore we must have it. But one is not to
question its nature, extent, value, or cost. In short, one
is not allowed to measure it.

If there can be equilibrium prices, there can be equilibrium quantities. Deviations from this norm, known
as gluts or shortages, are used to justify government
intervention in the markets. However, just because
one's offer to purchase gold at $10 an ounce elicits no
responses, one does not have grounds for concluding a
shortage of gold exists. Norms, or deviations from
these norms, have no basis in economic science.

Objective measure is absolutely fundamental to any
science. The law of supply and demand is a direct
attempt to subvert the need for measurement. It therefore removes economics from any consideration as a
science.

It is generally true that increasing the bid price for a commodity will bring more offers to sell it, and the inverse is true of the asked price. This is an empirical observation, but it is not always true. It is not a law of science. A law of science explains the actions of entities by a fundamental understanding of their nature. The entities being studied are human beings engaged in a specific type of economic behavior: monetary transactions. It is absurd to propose studying this behavior via the subjunctive measurement of non-existent transactions. It is absurd to propose a method for determining the "price of an object" when, in fact, a price is not the attribute of a good but of a transaction.

The law of supply and demand attempts to divorce economic activity from individual action. Hence no global context is ever made clear. Supply-demand analysis seems meaningful only if one is not clear whether one is referring to short-term or long-term, or whether one is referring to many traders or one trader, or whether one is referring to a specific existent, a group of similar goods, or all economic goods. The action to increase or decrease bid or asked prices is an individual action. The action to respond to these changes is also an individual action. Individuals make these actions for many different reasons and with many different planning horizons. One individual may raise the asking price of his product to squeeze the last nickel of revenue or profit from his customer over the next five minutes. Another individual with a longer planning horizon may lower his asking prices and increase the wages he pays his workers to create a wider market for his product in order to make efficient use of new production technology. The two cases cannot be integrated into the same supply-demand analysis for any such analysis must fail to take into account differences in individual action. No economists could use supply-demand methodology to produce an accurate analysis of the actions of real individuals trading real products in the real world. No such analysis has ever been offered; economists arbitrarily list a hypothetical example and let it go at that.

Economists today do not seriously offer the "law of supply and demand" as a practical method for determining actual prices of real transactions. Instead they use it to talk in unquantified terms about demand (or aggregate demand), with the usually unstated assumption that the government must somehow manage this entity to stimulate growth, prevent serious economic disequilibriums, or cure unemployment. The management of demand becomes the intellectual rationale for government intervention in the economy—i.e., the abrogation of property rights.

Any dollar spent by the government is a dollar taken from some individual, now or later. Hence, the government is an agent for distribution (specifically redistribution), and not an agent for the management of overall demand. It is axiomatic that one cannot distribute what has not yet been produced. Yet "the law of supply and demand" ignores this truth to justify government intervention.

Production, not demand, should be the primary focus of economics. We have seen how free trade facilitates production and how the correct use of monetary trade can make this process even more efficient. The "law of supply and demand" is the major attempt to subvert these economic realities.

Money, Credit, and Inflation

Nowhere in economic literature has there ever

appeared an adequate definition of money. Because
money provides the primary cardinal scale of measurement in economics, one can appreciate the disastrous implications of this lack of definition. The
results permeate all of economics, but the most serious
errors are the confusion of money and credit and the
lack of understanding of inflation.

Most attempts to define money are variants of "a
claim on wealth." This non-definition makes no distinction between money and credit; the two become
synonymous, a result which produces many invalid
conclusions.

First, economists conclude that banks create money,
the direct source of the notion that banks' credit activities should be regulated. Banks do not create money.
No economists would claim banks create gold, or
should be allowed to manufacture currency. Banks
create and trade in credit and, in so doing, create
wealth. The typical bank deals very little in cash, and
certainly does not create it.

Second, because monetary credit transactions have
an associated price, people who assume the equiva-
lence of credit and money (and who ascribe prices to
goods rather than to transactions), conclude that
money has a price, usually expressed in the form of an
interest rate. If the price of money is "too high," that is
"bad" for the economy, and this price must be regulated (or even worse nonsense, the "demand for money"
must be managed). In truth, money provides that
means to measure the size of monetary transactions,
their price.

Third, presumably because of the observed correla-
tion between the amount (face value) of credit outstanding and the overall size of the economy (for which
the GNP is a poor proxy), economists have created the
false doctrine of monetarism. It states that the com-

bined total of currency and some selected forms of
credit must be managed to grow at a rate roughly equal
to the "natural rate of growth of the economy." Among
other benefits, this approach supposedly controls
inflation. Aside from incorrect identification of the
nature of reality (money), the doctrine of monetarism
suffers from three false assumptions.

One, there exists no basis for the assumption of a
natural growth rate for the economy. This is yet
another example of economists' predilections for normative statements; on what basis does one discern
natural from unnatural growth? By natural, economists actually mean typical or historical (although we
will see that even this figure is not well-defined), and
offer no explanation as to why we should in future be
limited to historical growth, as opposed to whatever
growth we can achieve. No explanation as to why the
growth of the bastardized sum of money and credit
must be made to conform to this "natural rate of
growth" is attempted.

Second, there exists no rational or meaningful way
to "select the relevant forms of credit" one will include
in the aggregate sum of money and credit. The confusion of numerous measures results. The Federal Reserve
now publishes, among others, measures called M-1, the
Monetary Base, M-2, M-3, and L which measure various forms of credit. Obviously, the Fed does not know
what it is measuring, although that does not deter
monetarists from specifying what the target growth
rates for each measure should be.

Third, the confusion between money and credit leads
directly to the conclusion that credit, as well as money,
should be regulated. That this is in direct opposition to
most monetarists' professed preference for "free-market
economics" seems not to concern them. The syncretis-

tic outcome of monetarist policy is the direct control by government of all credit transactions, with an enormous opportunity cost of lost wealth. Worse, monetarism need not even control inflation. The total amount of currency is much smaller than the face value of outstanding credit: hence, large increases in currency can be buried in a moderate growth of "money plus credit." Taken to extreme, this can create an inflation-ridden recession.

The mechanics of this situation are worth investigating. Consider the case in which the amount of currency is held constant at $10 billion, and credit remains unregulated for one year. Suppose that the face value of outstanding credit at the beginning of the year was also $10 billion and that by year end the total of currency and credit had grown 5 percent, reflecting growth in the economy. Let us contrast this with the case in which the Federal Reserve lets the amount of currency expand 10% over the year and regulates credit so that the total of currency and credit grows 5% during the year. In doing the arithmetic, one finds that the Federal Reserve is required to restrict the growth of credit to zero. Can one conclude the economy should be flat, since no new credit has been created? No, the situation is far worse. For in creating 10% new currency, the Fed has shrunk the scale of measurement of money to 90.9% (100% divided by 110%) of its former size. While the outstanding credit remains constant in nominal terms, in real terms it has shrunk about 9%, with a negative effect on the economy. Monetarists reading this example will point out that the face value of outstanding credit is far larger than the amount of currency, so increases in currency do not much affect the allowable increase in credit. This is true, but only in nominal terms. For the change of monetary scale that currency increases produce means that, no matter what the ratio of outstanding credit and currency, if the percentage increase in currency is as large as or larger than the allowable percentage increase in nominal credit, the real amount of credit outstanding is constant or declines. (This is only true in an otherwise unregulated economy. Otherwise, some of the decrease may be offset by the introduction of new legal forms of credit that avoid regulation. However, to claim that such a situation represents management of the economy by monetarists is ludicrous. Even monetarists would not plan that one should count on the ability of banks to legally circumvent regulation when one is developing policy to "manage the economy.")

An offshoot of monetarist theory is something called the velocity of money. The velocity of money is calculated by dividing the GNP by the money supply (in reality, the total amount of money plus some forms of credit) to obtain a figure that supposedly represents how often each dollar was spent. Monetarists then claim that spending money more often will bid up prices, so one must be sure to watch the velocity of money when deciding how many dollars to print.

The velocity of money is meaningless. It is merely a poor ex post facto measure of the way people buy and pay for things. Its only significance is historical: Keynes felt that a relatively low velocity of money was one of the causes of the Great Depression. He proposed as a cure that government should take the public's money and spend it, because the public was not doing so. His conclusion is as false as the idea that the velocity of money is relevant. Currency does not get used up when spent. One may as well compute the velocity of height by computing the sum of everyone's height and dividing by the number of yardsticks in existence.

These errors—that banks create money, that money has a price, and that monetarism is valid—have a practical outcome: the present concept of a central bank—the Federal Reserve. Its ostensible purpose is to manage the money supply. Earlier it was shown that, in reality, this task belongs to Congress. The real purpose of the Fed is to eventually regulate all private credit transactions. The Fed conducts most of this regulation through private commercial banks and savings and loan associations. Its primary tools are the reserve requirement, the discount rate, and its open market operations. The details vary, but all are direct controls of the credit extended by or owned by banks, not that private financial institutions have been lax in their attempt to avoid control by inventing new forms of credit and legal organization. Recent innovations include: the appearance of bank-holding companies, the introduction of NOW accounts, and the spectacular success of money market funds and Eurodollar markets. A fascinating waltz takes place with private financial institutions and the Fed as unwilling partners. The often considerable lag in the introduction of regulations appropriate to some new form of credit allows financial institutions to make their profit before such innovations succumb to regulation. Already, NOW accounts are partially regulated (in the interest they pay), and the Fed has regulated, briefly, the entrance of funds into money markets. Other credit regulations also exist; for example, most states have usury laws that limit rates on consumer installment debt. In analyzing the Fed's actions, one should always keep in mind that the Fed's true objective is the control of all forms of private credit transactions. Those confused by recent moves of deregulation and tax cutting should recognize that the Administration has publicly stated that these moves are but a means to an end. The stated hope of the so-called supply-side economics is the rejuvenation of the American economy, *so that the government can have more money to spend*. Administration economists use the Laffer curve to calculate how to bleed the taxpayer most efficiently. Supply-side economics is tax policy, not economics. When it does not work, Congress will simply find another tax policy.

Money's lack of definition produces total confusion concerning the nature of inflation. No valid discussion of inflation exits anywhere. All such discussions make one or both of the following errors. Some equate inflation with the observed trends in the prices of all (or some) transactions. Others confuse money and credit.

The true cause of inflation is increases in the quantity of currency. The true effect of inflation is to increase the price of specific transactions over what they would have been had there been no inflation (in a free economy).

Economists who confuse price trends with inflation make the mistake of comparing the "price of goods" then and now. They conclude that these prices have been increasing (no explanation given) and thus inflation has occurred. Some specify certain target goods or services that are primary and cause the increased prices of other goods and services (as the increases work their way through the economy). Candidates include: wages, profits, oil, energy, housing, interest rates, and foreign exchange rates. Hence, people identify inflation as cost-push inflation, or as the result of wage-price spiral, and advocate price controls as the answer.

This totally false approach ignores completely the nature of money and price. Observing changes in the prices of similar transactions over time is pointless.

These can change for many reasons, including but not limited to: changes in the amount of currency, changes in people's preferences and tastes, changes in the nature of the goods themselves, new and more efficient production methods, and changes in the availability of raw materials. This approach also assumes that goods produced now are identical to those that were produced then, or else no basis of comparison is possible—a manifestly false assumption. To propose price controls as an answer is idiocy. A specific price occurs at a specific point in time; once it occurs, it is immutable for all time. To control prices one would have to rewrite history, for all prices are historical. What people actually mean when they speak of price control is simply the outlawing of certain transactions. Since traders will not continue to make transactions at a loss, trade will slacken and the only result is lost wealth.

Some economists go so far as to eliminate from consideration items that trade at volatile prices and speak of the "underlying, fundamental, or core" rate of inflation. With this approach, one can make inflation anything one wants, by selecting the right commodities for exclusion. One can point to the decreasing trend of prices in transactions involving buggy whips and conclude that we are in a period of deflation.

Even those who correctly avoid the issue of price increases between specific transactions by speaking of inflation as a "general rise in the overall price level" are mistaken. The implicit but unspoken assumption in that comparative statement is that prices today are to be compared to prices of yesterday. The correct comparison is, of course, to what these prices would have been had there been no increase in currency.

Economists who confuse money and credit produce a different set of fallacious conclusions about the nature and causes of inflation. They are concerned with the amount of money (actually money and credit) present—the quantity theory of money. In their view, price increases are caused by "too much money chasing too few goods," sometimes called "excess demand" (normal demand is not defined). The solution is either to control the amount of money (in reality regulate credit, usually by controlling its prices) or remove the "excess demand" via stiff taxes. Carried to extreme, either approach causes a recession, and ultimately a depression.

Economists who combine both of these mistakes concerning inflation reach conclusions not worth refuting.

Money is any fungible physical commodity with the following characteristics and used in the following way. An arbitrary but fixed physical amount (weight) of this commodity is assigned the value of one unit. The total amount of the physical commodity used as money must be fixed at "n" units, "n" normally being a large number. This commodity must have no intrinsic economic usefulness; its value stems only from its use as money, not from any other use. This commodity is then used as an objective scale of measurement to value transactions. Moreover, the amount of this commodity in anyone's physical possession serves to measure and account for the size of that person's general claim on other traders, exercised by the use of this commodity as a universal commodity in trade. The purpose of money is to measure objectively and account for each individual's general claim on other traders.

Credit is a promise to pay on the part of one trader to another. The promisee holds a promise to pay in lieu of the object promised. He extends credit to the promisor. A credit transaction is one involving credit—that is, involving a promise to pay.

A price is a measurement associated with a specific monetary transaction. Price measures the economic size of that transaction according to the scale of measurement provided by money.

Inflation is a measure of the rate of change of the scale of measurement that money provides, equal to the net increase of currency in a specific time period, usually expressed in percent per year.

Aggregate Behavior
(*The Non-Science of Macroeconomics*)

Macroeconomics concerns the measurement and management of a nation's economy, the aggregate trading behavior of all individuals taken as a whole. This subject receives more scrutiny by economists, by the press, by businessmen, and by anyone interested in politics or economic affairs in general than any other area of economics. It studies quantities such as the income level of a country, the employment or unemployment rate for the nation, and the inflation rate. Its ostensible purpose is to provide policy prescriptions that will succeed in moving these quantities to "desirable" levels. On a more grandiose level, macroeconomics attempts to integrate conceptually the economies of all trading nations and provide policy for the control and management of international trade and currency exchange.

Macroeconomics is devoid of any rational basis, fundamental truths, or claim to science. It is little more than a collection of inaccurate data, personal whims, and ad hoc, untested theories. There are few forecasters who actually believe in the numerology they produce, and there is certainly no one who can demonstrate a consistent record of accurate prediction. Yet no one

refrains from offering forecasts on interest rates, inflation, and GNP. (This is not to claim that any rational
economist would be able to accurately predict these
quantities; only that present predictions have no basis).
Those who practice macroeconomics are, in truth, political commentators and advisors whose prognostica-
tions bear little resemblance to reality and who prescribe policies with no regard for morality.

The reasons for this deplorable state of affairs are
twofold. One, economists have not deigned to study the
nature of man, the motor of all economic activity. Two,
economists have spared macroeconomics from the
rigors of the scientific method: data-gathering, hypothesis formulation, predictions by the hypothesis,
test by experimentation, hypothesis revision, and theory synthesis. This lack shows up clearly in the fact that
macroeconomics does not define rigorously a single
concept it purports to deal with.

A direct consequence of this lack of definition is the
lack of any appropriate scales of measurement. The
quantities mentioned above which macroeconomics
studies are, at best, inaccurate historical measurements, summed over time and measured with a scale
that changes over time. Consider the following specific
example.

At the end of each year, economists calculate two
measurements among others: nominal GNP and real
GNP. The first supposedly represents the total production of all economic activity for the nation, measured in
something called current dollars. The second supposedly measures the same quantity, taking into account
the change in the value of a dollar over the course of a
year. This change is taken into account in order that
year-to-year comparisons will be possible. Nominal
GNP is computed by adding up the prices of various

transactions over the course of the year. The specific transactions included are the final outputs for consumption, capital goods, and exports. The actual transactions chosen are irrelevant for the purposes of discussion; any set of transactions would do. (We will ignore the fact that not all transactions are reported to the government; hence, the figure is invalid before one starts. Estimates of this so-called underground economy have put it at a significant portion of the total economy—that is, larger than year-to-year changes in real GNP. We also ignore the fact that the scale of measurement for transactions has been changing continually over the year.)

Economists recognize that nominal GNP is not directly comparable to the previous year's figure, because of inflation. It conveys nothing to say that nominal GNP increased 10 percent from last year, until one knows what inflation is. If inflation was 5 percent, there was positive growth. If inflation was 15 percent, there was negative growth. Hence the next step is an attempt to adjust the nominal GNP to something called real GNP. This is done via a complicated price index, a comparison of the price of transactions this year (by category of good or service) to the price of transactions last year.

Observe the impossibility. Economists try to determine the values of two entities, actual price and change of scale of measurement, by observing the value of one variable, nominal price. They attempt to solve one equation with two unknowns, a mathematical impossibility. A concrete example will make this clear. One important class of transactions included in GNP calculations is consumption. Consumption accounts for between one-half and three-quarters of total GNP. Economists know the sum of money paid for consumption this year and the sum paid last year in nominal (current) dollar terms. They profess to have no a priori knowledge of the change of scale in money that has occurred over the year. How then can they compare the prices of these two sets of transactions? Only by making a subjective evaluation of what the goods consumed are actually worth. It is mathematically impossible to use this price data to determine both actual price and change of scale of measurement (a figure used for converting nominal GNP to real GNP) without making additional subjective evaluations concerning the worth of various economic goods and services. It is not possible to determine which part of the price change is due to real factors and which part is due to changes in the scale of measurement money provides. These can be determined only in conjunction with an understanding of the effect of currency increases.

One may argue that these subjective estimates are good and that the errors are small. However, it is not actual GNP that we are interested in, it is changes in actual GNP. This, by the economists' own figures, varies between approximately minus 5 percent and plus 5 percent. Thus, small subjective errors cause large percentage errors in the actual GNP increase or decrease which are large enough so that the figures are meaningless, no better than educated guesses.

In summary, concerning the measurement of GNP, we see that not only is the source of data inaccurate and incomplete, but there remains the fundamental impossibility of year-to-year comparison, if present methods are used, due to a changing scale of measurement of money.

Financial accountants have recognized the existence of this problem in preparing year-to-year financial statements for corporations. They are not remotely close to a solution, for their efforts to date are concentrated on price comparisons rather than fundamental questions concerning the appropriate scale of measurement.

Neither economists nor accountants have recognized the distinction between money and the prices paid for an economic good or service.

Macroeconomics' difficulties do not end here. Even if economists solve the problems of measurement that plague their analysis, the results would hold little value. They would show what had happened in aggregate but give no indication why. The figures are of no value in formulating policy. The escape from this apparent dilemma is to recognize that economists have no right to tell people what to do with their property. Their analysis is descriptive, not prescriptive, for economists have made no attempt to understand man, his mind, or how it makes economic decisions. Macroeconomic measurements are not something to be managed even if it were moral; they are a complex sum of numerous individual decisions. One cannot manage effects without understanding causes. Observing the sum result of a group's actions gives one neither the ability nor the right to "implement policy" to direct that group's actions towards "desirable" ends.

Macroeconomics reaches its zenith of pretentiousness in the development of complex mathematical models whose function is the simulation of the economy for the purpose of evaluating certain policies. With the considerable aid of computers, economists have developed hideously involved systems of econometric equations which supposedly predict the future. These models can contain hundreds of variables in hundreds of equations. Normally, these models are restricted to linear equations. In the special case of econometrics (mathematical modeling incorporating statistical uncertainty), linearity is an absolute requirement. No statistical analysis has yet been developed capable of handling higher-order functions.

Two kinds of variables appear in these equations: dependent and independent. Dependent variables represent the entities one wants to predict. Independent variables represent the observations one uses to make predictions. Let us ignore the considerable inaccuracy of measurement in the values of independent variables. The fallacy of such models is that these variables are somehow causal factors determining the values of the dependent variables. It is as if these models are constructed in isolation, for the effects of man, his inventions, innovations, decisions, and production are nowhere factored into the models. Naturally, the predictive abilities of these models reflect their faulty construction.

Statistics is properly used to detect patterns in a great deal of noise, for the purpose of creating or revising a scientific hypothesis. Once a hypothesis has been defined, one must use the scientific method of prediction, experiment, and testing to synthesize and prove a scientific theory. Statistics alone can never prove a scientific theory, it can only indicate whether a given hypothesis is a good candidate for testing. That statistical analysis is the only technique macroeconomics uses implies current macroeconomics can never discover any laws of science—and hence is not a science. The prevalent abuse and widespread misuse of statistical methodology indicates a callous indifference to truth on the part of macroeconomics.

In the previous example of econometric modeling, the appropriate use of statistics is as follows. (This is not to say the whole modeling approach is at all valid;

we are concerned here with statistical methodology.) One hypothesizes an elementary model with, say, three or four variables based on clear patterns in the observed data. One uses the experimental data to determine the various parameters and coefficients. One tests to see if this model provides a significant improvement in predictive ability over guessing. If so, it is considered valid. To increase the complexity and predictive power of such a model, one adds independent variables—one at a time. After each variable is added, one must test that it significantly increases the predictive power of the whole model. If econometricians adopted this approach, their models would cease growing at 10 or 15 variables. However, models involving 500 variables are eminently more prestigious and marketable; hence, their value cannot be questioned. They have nothing however to do with science.

Suppose one adopted this approach and created a statistically valid econometric method. What has one achieved? It is crucial to distinguish between a practical tool for business forecasting and a scientific theory.

A scientific theory identifies a law of nature, which in turn identifies the nature of existents. An econometric model integrates loose approximations and rough correlations. Its purpose is to provide an educated guess. The two entities do not belong in the same epistemological universe.

Econometricians may produce some results of practical use to the business community (although I have seen no evidence to date). It is vitally important to the future of economics that one understands that econometricians are not engaged in *science*.

This chapter discussed three specific areas in which economics suffers from a failure of analysis. These areas cover the breadth of modern economics and the roots of all economics. However, their significance is far greater than the invalidity of one particular science. Economic thought has a great influence on political practice. Incorrect theories in economics are translated into real policies that adversely affect individuals. The next chapter explores this subject.

The scientific mistakes common to all three areas of analysis are the failure to observe that man's mind is the motor of all economic activity and the failure to identify the correct scale of measurement for economic activity. These areas have invalidated practically all of modern economics.

Chapter Nine

Failures of Application

The intimate relationship between economics and politics translates mistakes in abstract economic theory into tangible failures of government. In particular, the failures of analysis just covered are the intellectual source of egregious political policy. Before investigating this situation in detail, it is useful to examine the connection between economics and politics.

In one of his all-too-rare rational and lucid moments Keynes wrote:

...the ideas of economists and political philosophers, both when they are right and when they are wrong, are more powerful than is commonly understood. Indeed, the world is ruled by little else. Practical men, who believe themselves to be quite exempt from any intellectual influences, are usually the slaves of some defunct economists. Madmen in authority, who hear voices in the air, are distilling their frenzy from some academic scribbler of a few years back. I am sure that that power of vested interest is vastly exaggerated compared with the gradual encroachment of ideas.[1]

This statement contains a profound truth. Keynes understood the power of ideas, making it doubly unfortunate that his were false.

Much direct evidence exists to support Keynes's claim. Adam Smith's book, *The Wealth of Nations*, published in 1776, was primarily a manifesto for free trade and individual liberty. (This is not an endorsement of Smith's book—it also contains much invalid economics.) Nine years later, the United States Constitution was written. Karl Marx's *The Communist Manifesto* appeared in 1848. It provided the dubious intellectual justification of a worker's revolt. Sixty-nine years later, after many unsuccessful revolts throughout Europe, these ideas reached fruition in the October Revolution in Russia.

On a less revolutionary scale, Keynes's writings of the 1920s and 1930s were partly responsible for the New Deal legislation enacted during the Great Depression. The current monetarist experiments in Britain and the United States owe much to Milton Friedman's ideas.

---

[1] J.M. Keynes, *The General Theory* (Cambridge, England: Macmillan Press, 1975), p. 383.

In all cases, economic theory provided the moral and intellectual ammunition that politicians and revolutionaries needed to justify their positions and actions. In their political metamorphosis, economic ideas exert tremendous influence over the ordinary citizen. What then is the consequence of invalid economic theory?

Economic theory manifests itself politically in either legislation affecting property or political entities with the right to make decisions concerning private property. Concrete examples of the former are: wage and price control, fiscal policy, and antitrust law. An example of the latter is the Federal Reserve. Each of these represent the legal form of an invalid economic idea.

Any rational buyer, all else being equal, prefers a lower price to a higher price. Hence, legislating prices downward has enormous political appeal. Without appropriate economic justification, a politician has no means of marketing this powerful tool for buying votes. Fortunately for the politician, economists provide much putatively objective justification. First, by ascribing prices to goods rather than transactions, economists portray price as an ongoing, manageable attribute of goods rather than a fixed measurement of a particular transaction. Hence, economists falsely conclude that price control is feasible. Second, the false supply-demand model of price determination provides a methodology of price control: management of prices toward the so-called (but unmeasurable) equilibrium price. Third, by portraying inflation as both bad and caused by increases in the "price of goods," economists provide politicians with a moral rationale to control prices. These three false economic ideas result directly in wage and price control. Its practitioners are blind to the fact that it has never worked. It is no more than the outlawing of certain transactions—a direct, legal impediment to trade. Its only result is the loss of wealth that would otherwise have been obtained.

Fiscal policy, also known as macroeconomic policy or management of aggregate demand, is a doctrine based on the belief that it is both possible and right for the Federal Government to manage the whole economy to achieve "desirable ends." In reality, it is direct government involvement in economic affairs. The government abrogates the individual's right to property by making economic decisions enforced by law concerning the property of private citizens. Examples are numerous: transfer payments (the purchase of A's vote, financed by property stolen from B); provision of economic services by the government—such as the post office and public schools—on the grounds that they are somehow essential or necessary; subsidization of certain industries that are politically attractive and economically unviable, such as synfuels; cut-rate financing for large corporations such as Chrysler and Lockheed in order to keep or "create jobs"; and direct regulation of trade (FCC, FTC, ICC, DOE, etc.) on no grounds whatsoever. The common element in these examples is the partial or complete removal of decision-making concerning his property from the individual. These decisions are then made by disinterested second parties for irrelevant motivations. The benefits of the decisions are extolled and the costs ignored. The biggest cost is the foresaking of the principle of property rights, with a concomitant opportunity cost in lost wealth creation. No mention is made of the fate of the stolen property had it not been stolen. Politicians object to tax reductions as a subsidy of the rich, equating not stealing your money with subsidizing you. The very concept of macroeconomic policy directly conflicts with property rights. Both cannot exist simultaneously. Property rights have the decided advantage of morality.

Antitrust law, which regulates the economic activity of large companies, has its economic origins in the invalid concept of perfect competition. Perfect competition[2] is defined in terms of supply-demand functions, and hence has no scientific basis. Politicians wield terms such as oligopoly, monopoly, cartel, price-fixing, and perfect competition and then manufacture laws containing these terms. Yet there does not exist a single politician who could define these terms, for in the context of economics all are invalid concepts: incorrect identifications of reality. A few simple economic fallacies magnified by the power of the legislative process produce profound negative results. The unfortunate fact perpetuating this situation is that the average American has no way to identify what he no longer has an opportunity to possess; he does not know what could have been.

One can see antitrust laws are devoid of meaning, and therefore can be arbitrarily enforced at the whim of those in political power, if one tries to apply these laws to any actual case. Antitrust laws forbid combinations in restraint of trade, a proscription without meaning. If Exxon acquired Mobil or IBM acquired ATT, the Justice Department would certainly challenge these combinations as restraint of trade—and do so on no objective basis. "Concentration of business" or "combined market share" may be deemed "too large," but the Justice Department will not and cannot provide a standard to measure against, nor an expla-

---

[2] When economists speak of competition, the fact in nature they have unsuccessfully identified is the existence of economic alternatives.

nation of why the Government should be concerned
with a company's market share. The Government cannot define restraint of trade, nor point to a single
example in its successful Sherman Antitrust Act
prosecutions. Take, for example, the 1937 Alcoa case.
After losing at the District Court level, the Government
appealed to the Circuit Court of Appeals on the grounds
that, regarding the charge of monopolization, the District Court had incorrectly identified the relevant
market and therefore its market-share calculations
were wrong. By redefining the market, the Appeals
Court convicted Alcoa of monopolization, a breach of
the Antitrust Act. In fact, Alcoa was a hugely successful, productive, competitive enterprise that obtained its
market leadership through innovation and industry.
No specific act of illegality was ever alleged or identified. The Government contended only that Alcoa's
"share of market" was "too large." The definitions of
"market" and "too large" are protean and readily
adapt to the political purpose at hand. Alcoa's crime
was simply to be successful. The psychological origin
of such a charge is envy and its motive is power lust.
Incompetents have always been envious of the effica-
cious, but these puerile emotions remain impotent
while without political manifestation.

In this one can see the origin of antitrust law: the
desire for political control of corporations as a remedy
for failure to obtain economic control in a free market.
And in so doing, the Government burdened the individual with exactly what these laws were said to prevent: restraint of trade. For the only meaningful use of
the term restraint is coercive restraint. The Government and only the Government can coercively fix
prices, coercively protect monopolies, coercively limit
production, and coercively ration goods. Try to estab-

lish a new electric power utility or a new local telephone company, try to sell natural gas below its regulated interstate price, or try to import Japanese cars in excess of the official quota, and you will quickly learn the real meaning of trade restraint.

The Federal Reserve results directly from the confusion of money and credit. Had economists been able to correctly identify the nature of money, the Federal Reserve would not exist. However, it does exist and it regulates a large portion of outstanding private credit. The Federal reserve has lately been enamored of the false doctrine of monetarism, resulting in the effective camouflaging of the true cause of inflation. The Federal Reserve is not concerned with the money supply; Congress tells the Federal Reserve how many dollars to print. The true goal of the Federal Reserve is the regulation of private credit. The Federal Reserve has not even bothered to explain the supposed advantages of such a policy.

From its inception, the Fed has produced detrimental results. After its 1913 creation, the Fed busied itself providing below-market credit to banks. Banks are merely financial intermediaries; to use cheap credit, they were compelled to market it in marginal and dubious channels—for example, stock market speculators who bought on margin. This practice contributed to the speculative stock market bubble in the late 1920s. A crash was ineluctable.

Today the Fed has political control over the lifeblood of a capitalist society: its currency. By deliberately confusing money and credit, it has obtained political control over the credit markets. Chronic banking crises, Third World debt instability, and the ability of Congress to achieve trillion-dollar debt result.

As these four examples indicate, economists must

bear a fearsome responsibility for the practical results of their errors. All four stem from a common root.

Economists have failed to identify the nature and source of the individual's right to property. Economists have ignored that man's very nature requires, in order that he survive as a human, that each individual must own and be responsible for his property. Property is man's essential physical connection to reality. No moral or intellectual support exists for the extortion of private property by the state. Practically all modern intellectuals ignore the fact that no other so-called human rights are possible without the right to property and that the atrocities of Hitler's and Stalin's regimes were caused by exactly the same view of man as that which leads to the denial of the right to property: the refusal to regard each man as an independent, decision-making entity with a right to life.

The terrible result is the endorsement of statist (non-capitalistic) forms of government: political systems in which the State has a "right to property" and so is allowed to extort private property. Decisions regarding property are made by the State—in practice, this means by a powerful elite. Do not be confused by references to different forms of statism: communism, socialism, or mixed economies. Do not be misled by the assertion that statism is moral as long as it is democratic. Democratic forms of statist government merely postpone the day of final collapse, for its leaders are limited in action to what is politically expedient, to what will get them reelected. The motor behind the encroachment of State power is false economic and philosophic ideas (more exactly, the lack of the right ideas), a motor independent of democracy. Democracy is not a form of political organization; it is a method of choosing leaders. The issue is whether the State has the right to property or whether individuals do. And it is strictly an either-or issue—no middle ground exists.

What moiety of your property shall we allow the State to take? Whatever it can get away with is the only conceivable result of the apostasy which does not recognize man's right to property, and the practical and observed outcome of such a policy.

Today, the "state of the economy" means the economics of the State.

One sets a precedent in allowing the State to make any economic decisions without the voluntary cooperation of each individual involved. Every disruption or failure arising from regulated trade, legal monopoly, or direct economic activity on the part of the State justifies further efforts and programs to "correct" this failure. The primary defense against such expansion, the principle of property rights, has already been abandoned.

Transferring the decision-making process from the individual to the State poses a grave danger. A state is not an integral entity with coherent, unified goals and policies. It is a collection of individuals pursuing power politics, and its actions concerning property are irrational and erratic. The individuals who bear the effects of those decisions are not those who make them. An individual who cannot feel pain will soon die. A state which does not bear the cost of its actions will suffer the same fate.

The State exists solely to secure the human rights of the citizens it governs. Human rights concern the relationship amongst men and the management of individual men's competing claims on nature. The State's charge is to protect man from violence initiated by others, be they other individuals or foreign states, and to protect man's method of survival by protecting his

right to property. The method granted to the State to
perform this duty is a legal monopoly of the use of force:
the legislators, the police, and the courts. These principles are absolute and intransigent; there are no
exceptions.

Specifically the State is not directly responsible for
the economic well-being of its citizens; such a charge is
beyond its physical capacity. Nor do there exist the
State's rights, only the state's obligations—the obligation to secure the rights of all individuals by the use of
force against those individuals who violate the rights
of others.

The Constitution of the United States was man's
noblest attempt to codify these principles into law, a
cynosure for the civilized world. It attempted to limit
the powers of government and create a government of
law, not men; a final, objective arbiter of social dispute.
The Constitution, while brilliant in concept, failed in
execution. The authors made two mistakes. They ne-
glected, for political reasons, to apply its principles to
all men; slaves were excluded from its protection.
Second, the Constitution failed to make the right to
property an absolute, inalienable right. With property
not inviolate, the State moved quickly to take control of
it (see especially the Sixteenth Amendment).

These Constitutional errors have produced a semi-
socialist country in which one's right to property has
been steadily eroded, one's right to life is directly
abjured by the draft, and equality has supplanted liberty as a political objective—equality without reference
to any standard. America is losing the notion of political liberty. Freedom requires a context. To be free, one
must be free of something. In a capitalistic society, one
is free of coercive interference in one's life and property. In modern America, freedom means free of eco-

nomic cost. One becomes free of hunger via food stamps, free of the elements via government shelters, free of the need to conduct a productive existence via welfare, and free of the need to plan via social security.

Today the only country with any hope of a long-term future is the United States, and the only mechanism to insure that future is a new constitution that explicitly secures the right to property for all men. The United States should take pride in the fact that it is the only nation in all of history in which such a radical change has a possibility, albeit a small one, of being achieved by nonviolent means.

The new constitution should formally affirm and secure the rights of all individuals: life, liberty, and property. These rights are inalienable; they derive, not from a Creator, but from man's very nature as a rational being with free will. As such, they are inseparable from man, part of his being. To be without the right to life, liberty, or property is to not be.

A change as drastic as a new constitution will not occur until men re-examine their fundamental philosophic convictions. Clearly the time required is measured, not in years, but in generations.

The executive, legislative, and judicial branches of government require real resources in order to operate. Politicians must be paid, armies equipped. Yet the nature of property rights forbids that these economic needs be satisfied via taxes (nonvoluntary contributions). The American revolutionary cry, "no taxation without representation," was two words too long. The only moral source of government financing is voluntary contributions.

Before this solution is summarily dismissed as unworkable and preposterous, two observations need be made. One, the current popular objections to taxes stem from their confiscatory nature. In the United States, governments account directly for over 40% of all economic activity and severely regulate most of the remaining. The scale of government is stupendous. A state whose only responsibility was the prevention of violence and maintenance of property rights would be smaller than current levels by at least an order of magnitude. Hence the voluntary contributions required to maintain such a government would be miniscule compared to current tax levels. Two, men responsible for their own existence tend to behave rationally. The stability and security inherent in a free, rational, capitalistic state are enormous—much greater than have ever existed anywhere. Throughout history, men have always sought freedom to the extent they often paid for it with their lives, for many felt life on other terms was not worth living. Throughout history, men have voluntarily paid for value received, and the value of such a state is greater than any individual has ever achieved, save in fiction. Men with extensive amounts of property would contribute greater amounts to the State, for they have a bigger economic stake in maintaining order. (This is an observation of facts in reality; no moral conclusion is implied.) However, all men have an equal moral stake.

To most, adducing voluntary contributions as the sole means of supporting government probably appears ludicrous. Perhaps this will lead these people to reconsider the nature of the government they are now involuntarily supporting, and to consider the enormous value of one they would voluntarily support.

A state which drafts its protectors and extorts its financing admits directly and openly its lack of merit. It has no long-term future, for one day it will run out of victims. There has never existed a shortage of people who volunteered to protect any semi-worthwhile political organization. Man's choice is to identify the correct nature of government or perish, for reality cannot be faked.

In a free society, the following would be absent: public schools, public transportation, public utilities, public communications facilities, socialized medicine, subsidized art, government post offices, antitrust laws, trade regulation, banking regulation, wage or price controls, income tax, sales tax, subsidized housing, affirmative action, censorship, draft boards, public parks, union rights, public welfare, government unemployment insurance and social security, government job-creation programs, etc.

One cannot conclude there would be no schools, medicine, pension plans, or unemployment insurance. These services are a great value and people would willingly pay for them. The cry that some people would not be able to afford their "rightful" level of services is an excuse to justify legal theft from the productive and an attempt to subvert the right to property. Perhaps all that these individuals need do is adjust their priorities from cars and clothes to medicine and education. Remember, they are no longer involuntarily buying rocket ships to the moon, expensive wars in the Southeast, or featherbedding bureaucrats. Perhaps this newfound purchasing power will cover their needs. If not, perhaps they would be motivated to do something beyond complaining and seeking a free ride. Somebody currently pays for these services unwillingly and should do so no longer.

Economics will progress only when economists discern the need for and identify the nature of the right to property. To date, this has not happened. To date, economics is not a science.

There exists a positive side to the problems discussed here. Correct economic theory, as well as bad economic theory, can be translated to political reality. The necessary precondition is the identification of correct economic theory.

Appendix

Economists subscribing to the theory of marginal utility may object to the feasibility of A's evaluating his possessions by the method of Chapter Three. Von Mises[1] showed the impossibility of objectively measuring what he terms subjective use value—that is, defining a new unit, the util, to serve as a standard to measure subjective use value. Before answering this objection, it is necessary to describe the theory of marginal utility.

Carl Menger[2] rightly observed that value is not

---

[1] *The Theory of Money and Credit* (Liberty Classics, 1980), p. 55ff.

[2] *Principles of Economics* (NYU Press, 1976), p. 116.

139

inherent in goods per se, nor a property of them, but
rather a function of the relationship between men and
goods. Value is meaningless outside the context of
man. Menger further observed that in general the
value per unit a man ascribes to specific goods decreases
as the amount of that good he possesses increases. He
values further units of the good less highly than the
first units. The marginal utility[3] of additional units
decreases as the amount of a given commodity one
possesses increases because the first units are sufficient to satisfy one's most pressing needs. Menger uses
his theory of marginal utility to explain why economiz-
ing individuals engage in trade—namely, the differing
marginal utilities derived by individuals from the
same good due to differing circumstances. (As shown
in Chapter Two, this is not the prime cause of trade in a
modern economy—it applies mostly to what Menger
calls goods of the first order.) The exchange enables
each to attain a higher marginal utility. Marginal utility analysis leads Menger to distinguish between the
use value and exchange value of a good: the use value
being appropriate to a good one wishes to use directly,
the exchange value being appropriate to a good one
wishes to trade.

These two values are related by marginal utility
functions which give the decreasing marginal utility
derived by individuals from increasing units of a good.
Because the specific nature of these functions is undefined (other than their monotonic decreasing nature),
Von Mises was able to show the impossibility of an

---

³ This theory would be better named one of marginal value, but
marginal utility is the common usage, perhaps because value is an
overworked word with meanings both within and outside economics. For Menger, a thing possesses utility simply if it has the (possibly unrealized) capacity to satisfy a human need.

absolute cardinal measure for subjective use value; i.e., there is no natural unit for measuring this entity. This result is a direct mathematical consequence of the undefined nature of the marginal utility function. How then can one insist that A evaluate his possessions?

The precise kind of measure asked of A must be defined. Von Mises distinguished two kinds: ordinal measure, in which one ranks items as first, second, third, etc.; and cardinal measure, in which one compares entities quantitatively to a standard defined unit—e.g., the inch. Ordinal measure is very rough; it gives no comparative information about the various entities other than their relative rank. And, as Von Mises showed, cardinal measure is inappropriate for A.

However, two distinct kinds of cardinal measure can be distinguished. First is absolute cardinal measure, the quantitative comparison to an objectively defined unit: length in feet, time in seconds, etc. Second, called proportional cardinal measure, is the relative comparison of different entities without the additional comparison to a standard unit. This measure is inferior in information to absolute cardinal measure but superior to mere ordinal measure. By arbitrarily fixing A's total of value, one forces A to make proportional comparisons. Because no objective standard unit has been defined, the resultant numbers considered individually have no objective significance to B. However, these numbers convey more information than ordinal ranking; comparison of two measurements gives a proportional evaluation.

Indeed, absolute cardinal measure may be considered a special case of proportional cardinal measure in which an objectively defined fixed unit is always used for the comparison. Why then can we not derive an absolute cardinal measure unit for value? The answer lies in the nature of economic value. It is neither intrinsic, residing solely in the good itself, nor subjective, determined strictly at A's whim, but is objective and dependent on the relationship between A and the good. Substituting B for A changes the relationship and therefore the measurement of value.

Theoreticians of marginal utility may claim that, in the absence of money—and hence price—and in the absence of other traders, A would be unable to make such refined measurements of his possessions. However, they impart the same capabilities to A by assuming he can in his own mind measure the marginal utility of additional commodity units. For while, in a theoretical discussion of value, marginal utilitarians never identify any specific functions of marginal utility, it is implicit in A's or a trader's actions that he be able to quantify his marginal utility in order to make economic calculations; otherwise, he would not know when to stop producing if in isolation nor trading if in a barter economy.[4] It is possible to make proportional cardinal measurements without any implied standard unit—that is, in the absence of absolute cardinal measure. One can know that rod A is three times the length of rod B without knowing the length of either in inches, meters, or cubits. Hence, the existence of A's proportional measurements does not imply any objective standard unit, nor does it imply that those measurements considered individually have any absolute objective relevance to B nor to B's evaluations.

The source of A's evaluations is his ability to interpret conceptually the world around him. A can conceive of the relationship between his possessions and his survival. A is not required to quantify his posses-

---

[4] *Principles of Economics*, p. 183.

sions into arbitrary bushels, pounds, loaves, or barrels. Instead, A evaluates each possession as an integral unit and considers alternately his possession or non-possession of same. No question of *marginal* utility arises. His evaluations measure his possessions in a relative manner—they do not assign value to various autonomous goods. His evaluations apply only to the situation as it is—his position with respect to nature. They do not consider the possibility of additional amounts of specific possessions, nor the possibility of trade. His ability to evaluate is a consequence of his rationality—to deny it is to deny that rationality.

The analogy of Chapter Three, comparing A's evaluation of his possessions and the case of money in a monetary economy, illustrates the importance of the scheme of proportional measure. Objectivity arises when monetary transactions take place—the transition from proportional cardinal measure to absolute cardinal measure. The existence of the transaction relates the value judgments of A and B and enables them to objectify the measurement—according to the scale of money. We *define* the dollar as $1/n$ of the total money. The dollar becomes the objective standard unit whereby all traders can evaluate the price of a given transaction and compare it to their own positions. The lack of such transactions is precisely why no such absolute cardinal measure can be imposed on the imaginary util.

The epistemological problem in economics is the measurement of economic value. Classical economics provides the quantity theory of money, which compares the total "amount" of money to something called the price level. More precisely it compares changes in the amount of money to changes in the price level of goods. Von Mises extended the Austrian School of

Economics into the monetary realm by applying the concept of individual action (as opposed to societal action) as a technique to analyze money. Accepting the theory of marginal utility, he was able to show the impossibility of objective measurement of subjective use value. He recognized the difficulties this caused for the objective measurement of exchange value and ducked the issue by ultimately deriving what he called the objective exchange value of money from historical transactions adjusted by complicated variational processes. Von Mises (as well as the classical economists) never adequately defined money per se; he merely expounded on the so-called different types of money: fiat money, commodity money, credit money, etc. He seems to have realized the confusion this caused for objective exchange values, but never resolved the problem.[5]

The common error these approaches make is the attribution of price to units of goods per se. The error is direct in classical economics and indirect in the Austrian school—being implicit in the theory of marginal utility. Rational Economics avoids the problem by assigning the measurement of price to transactions and doing so in a very specific way: via the use of the monetary mechanism. By making price measurement inherent in the transaction, Rational Economics avoids the issue of what other amounts of the transacted commodity traders may own, and thereby the entire issue of marginal utility. Rational Economics regards the fact of marginal utility as a truism (cf. the discussion of the law of supply and demand in Chapter Eight), not as an economic law nor as the means of economic calculation. Rational Economics regards

---

[5]   *The Theory of Money and Credit*, p. 173

marginal utility as an incorrect perspective for economic analysis. Value depends on the relationship of a specific man to specific goods. One can assign value in a proportional manner to the specific goods one owns. In a monetary trading system, one can assign price to specific transactions. One cannot combine these measurements and produce an objective value or price for goods per se. The attribution of price and therefore value to goods per se directly contradicts the fact that value can arise only in the context of man. Doing so forced the Austrian School economists to derive many types of value (subjective use value, objective use value, objective exchange value, etc.) and many types of money (fiat, commodity, credit, money substitutes, etc.). The attribution of price to transactions encounters no such difficulties.

Despite this error of method, the contribution of the Austrian School is very great, for it was the first to shift economists' perspective from the economic system as a whole to the actions and wills of independent individuals. A desire to isolate the elements of economic activity caused this shift. It is unfortunate they did not also shift from "goods involved in trade" to transactions. For not only do goods have value only in the context of man, specific goods have specific price only in the context of specific men undertaking specific actions.